Beating Tantra
at Its Own Game
Spiritual Sexuality

Beating Tantra at Its Own Game
Spiritual Sexuality

by

Arthur Lytle, Ph.D.

FALCON PRESS
LAS VEGAS

International Standard Book Number: 0-941404-89-7

First Edition 1989
By Falcon Press

Book Design, Typography and Production by
RapidScribe Communications
A division of
Studio 31/Royal Type
27 West 20th Street • Room 1005
New York, NY 10011

Cover Painting by Sallie Ann Glassman
Cover Design by Studio 31

FALCON PRESS
1209 South Casino Center, Suite 147
Las Vegas, Nevada 89104
1-702-385-5749

Manufactured in the United States of America

Contents

Acknowledgments

This work was made possible by the experience, sacrifices, support, and love of my wife Lora, Dr. Donald R. Schaffer, Dr. Cecil Osborne, Max Heindel, Rev Trudy Jarno, Rev. Opal Kieth and to several companions from other lifetimes who are still teaching me about Life and Love.

The lion's share of my gratitude goes to the unlimited Patience, Wisdom and Love of our Guides and Elder Brothers of the celestial Hierarchy known to me as "The T. George Group," for Their encouragement. Their skilled guidance and counsel have here done almost literally the impossible, in enabling us humans to have Life and to have it more abundantly.

Dedication

"Classical Yoga and Christianity share in common the concept and approach of fighting to overcome the evils of the lower or sexual nature on the pathway to becoming a Master of Life.

"Tantra Yoga, on the other hand, approaches the Eternal Trek through integrating and mastering the human need for acceptance and love through mastery of that so-called lower nature, thus attaining self-mastery on the way to that same Mastery of Life.

"Tantra Yoga does not advocate promiscuity, nor exploitation of one human of another. When a person masters the sensual aspect of love, the expression of love by orgasm may diminish, may be found unnecessary, a higher affinity then being expressed but transcended by higher expression of affinity.

"We dedicate this, our collection of instructions for attainment of your consummate happiness, that you shall put forth every effort to build your love nature, experiencing its highest potentials. Such dedication shall be well rewarded.

"May our mutual efforts be well received."

Why Another Sex Book?

"Why do we offer another book on Sex, when so many are already on the market? We have good reason, as you can soon judge for yourself.

"Probably the most popular forms of pleasurable involvement available via the human appetites are those concerning eating and sex. In accord with one's health and opportunity, the next most popular forms of raw human sensual indulgence include drinking, games and fighting, deriving strong feelings of power and pleasure by inflicting pain on others . . . often the uglier the better.

"Now, it is well known that among persons unable to maintain positions of control over others through normal sexuality, those whose physical appetites are no longer capable of being sated through direct sexual intercourse, usually retain strong emotional feelings. Some them seek satisfaction through sadomasochism, through inflicting pain on themselves and/or their partners, even while going through the rituals of sexual intercourse. Through Time, we have then insight into degraded forms of sexual activity used to attain the fundamental sense of aliveness.

"We introduce a little-known form of gaining supreme pleasure that is seldom explored, being gained by combining Sexuality with Spirituality. As current literature could affirm, that little known route to ecstasy is called Tantra Yoga. The benefits of Tantra Yoga become available as persons overcome their lower appetites. They learn to master certain energy flows. Practiced at its heights, they become able to direct their attention to what occurs in the finer essences in the soul and spirit of the participating male and female partners.

"We describe here an opportunity to explore, develop, and qualify for the promise of the highest that male-female intercourse can provide. We offer an adventure that promises to gain, for successful practitioners a repeatable experience permanently transcendent over anything in the usual human experience.

"Greatest satisfaction is available to persons who early in life have recognized and put into effect the opportunity to experience what Tantra Yoga can provide, especially in their later years, for those persons whose parallel interest in spiritual development has become their primary focus.

"We introduce an approach available to anyone interested enough to undertake the processes of perfecting total human development, combining personality development with the processes for attaining the highest in human spiritual development. One then attains to that Love which passeth all understanding, then experiencing a male-female relationship knowable otherwise only to the gods . . . indeed at times exceeding that, because the gods do not have flesh!"

Preface

"How could anything be better than good old Adam and Eve sex?

"What more could there possibly be?

"How can you use Tantra Yoga and Spirituality in the same sentence?

"Isn't any kind of Yoga a sidetrack for the spiritual aspirant?

"Important questions all. From OUR point of view they are interrelated. We address them here because the answers include the major reasons why so many people are so deeply dissatisfied with their present relationships. By clarifying the issues we proffer ways for you to resolve your dilemmas and transform your love life.

"We present Tantra Yoga as a way to raise the limited conventional pleasures of the flesh to levels of Bliss vaguely suspected. To avoid consequences of unbalanced psychic development, special exercises are described to open the chakras.

"More than being another commentary on Sexual Technology, our purpose is to provide ways to develop the total person, and to merge Sexuality with Spirituality, yielding a more perfect and greater Love, a Love that fulfills, that has MEANING . . . combining PURPOSE for LIVING with PURPOSE for LOVING. That objective is made available by perfecting both the human mind and the human body, thus awakening the consciousness to the subtle psychic currents flowing within the human structure.

"Such personal transformation may seldom be accomplished in a short time, but this book will surely transform one's enjoyment of Life, and can greatly enhance personalizing the Love of the Masters.

"For persons who are still squeamish on the propriety of The Hierarchy issuing such a volume, we find these contents supportive of Jesus' claim "I come that you might have Life and have it more abundantly," and "Be ye transformed by the renewal of your mind." [KJV John chapter 10:10 and Romans chapter 12:2]"

Foreword

"You do not have to give up Sexuality to have Spirituality. In fact, if you will make the effort advanced here to master yourself, you can experience the best of *both* worlds.

"By producing this book, the Invisible Hierarchy of Elders and Guides offers Humanity a rare opportunity for self-mastery through and beyond Tantra Yoga. A part of our ministry in working for The Christ is to offer specific counsel and instruction to anyone who cares enough to realize his highest potential to follow through on this open invitation.

"To experience one's incarnate pleasures and potentials requires perfecting his health, overcoming his addictions, and revising his subconscious or ego-self programming and attitude systems. One rises above the need for celibacy in its traditional sense by mastering one's self-built Psychic Self-Defense Department, the personality self and its subconscious devil-like patterns which control a person's reactions to the pressures of Earth life. One comes to understand *true* love, shedding dependency on compulsive social relationships or addictions, becoming *able* to share in the experience of joy transcendent. The through-the-veil ministry we offer here is oriented that you shall share Life with us in the Higher Dimensions as a conscious co-worker incarnate among your fellow Earthlings.

"Preparing yourselves for being a channel and co-worker usually means establishing a new set of priorities. Having been attracted to this book, you are of above intelligence. Hence, you in particular are encouraged to investigate our ministry, easily understanding why we are *willing* to help you undergo the personal transformation required to implement our suggested Life Program.

"For Spiritualizing your Sexuality, your enjoyment of male-female relationships will far surpass the "good times" frequently sought and sometimes experienced, while yet mastering—spiritualizing—your Self.

"Our present work offers you through-the-veil coaching in personal transformation. Holistic by nature, our program integrates technologies derived from Religion, Metaphysics, Meditation, Psychology, Psychotherapy, Psycho-Kinesiology (tm), and other avant-garde practices called the Healing of Memories, Rolfing, Primal Therapy, Reiki, NLP, Regression, etc.

"In this book we are restoring portions of the Ancient Mysteries into contemporary language, fulfilling the Jesus Christ message that through the Perfected Love relationship, the human Prodigal Son initiates and completes the classical trip home to the The Father's House.

"As to our identity and credentials, suffice it to know that our most recent incarnations are referenced in the archives and journals of a hundred years ago, still highly respected in the political, scientific, and medical/psychiatric dominions of today. For a while longer we prefer to remain incognito, as little is to be gained by revealing who we were in our most recent incarnations. We prefer that you heed the *message*, rather then following through with it merely because of the title or high rank we might have held. We have overcome the world, have become christed, and are now working to implement the teachings of Our Master Jesus of Nazareth. We are recruiting and training co-workers on His behalf.

"In summary, for achieving Self Mastery, you can have it all! But stand by, as we guide you in how to do it."

CHAPTER

1

Definitions

"Our definitions may extend conventional interpretations of words, which in our realms and in Aquarian Age society may necessarily assume broader meanings. As a result of using our expanded definitions, persons can find release from the limited aspect of living, rising into the more responsible and more enjoyable Universe, to the extent they become able to understand properly the *concepts* behind the words used to describe their relationships in and assessments of Life."

1. What is Tantra Yoga?

"Tantra Yoga is a collection of ancient yogic practices which may be lumped under the name TANTRISM. It had its origins in the search for superhuman power through invocation of spells, formulas, rites and the like. The principle concern in practicing Tantra Yoga became the machination of sexual magic. Use of mantras became a sort of magical language, believed to be effective on divine levels, and to cultivate and develop higher levels of personal divinity. Accumulation of such skills indeed produced superhuman sexual power. Contemporary resurrection of certain lower levels of tantric practice has been effective in diverting attention from long-term spiritual development into short-term attainment of sexual gratification and glorification. While nothing is really wrong with taking advantage of side benefits from increased libido, it is believed that making sexual magic an end in itself is a bastardization of a spiritual practice, and doomed to produce deterioration of the higher mental and soul processes of said adherents and practitioners. One purpose of this treatise is, then, to restore the original principles and purposes of Tantra Yoga as a powerful method for Self Realization, of which sexual power is a step along the way, or only fallout, but one to be found less satisfactory than full Self Realization, which includes but goes beyond Tantra Yoga."

2. How do YOU define SEXUALITY?

"Sexuality, as We use the term, is distinct from sensuality. Sexuality is one form of polarity, as such is a key part of Universal Creativity. In different activities it takes different yet familiar forms, like black and white, up and down, on and off, wet and dry, light and dark, and others that may come to mind. Polarity is a fundamental fact of Life as the dipole is for Physics and Chemistry. The spiritual dipole of sexuality appears familiarly as the male-female current flow noted in Tantric Sex, and as the Healer's current flows in Spiritual Healing. Sensuality, as we use the term, is actually the search for the pleasures produced by sexual relationships.

"Human intercourse or sexuality on all levels is evident only as a small tip of an eternal iceberg, and whatever one's adjustment to it is likely to be found reflected in his or her overall adjustment to the Flow of Life in the Cosmos, also on all levels. Success in Life depends on one's ability to recognize 'The Flow' and to work with it."

3. What is Love, if not Sex?

"Throughout Time, Love has had many definitions, not feasibly reviewed here. However, one key facet important to Us is that Love brings joy into another person's life, without strings, without expectations, and does not at all need orgasms, aphrodisiacs, alcohol, moonlight, drugs, or gifts for its expression. The intensity of sexual intercourse can indeed be heightened by the presence of Love, but Love is expressible on ALL levels in the Cosmos. Love as sexual intercourse is experienced only in Matter.

"Sex, not Love, is used as a temporary palliative to assuage the pressures of frustration, as a reward, as a medium of exchange, as when a female wants something a male can procure for her . . . perhaps a meal or a roof . . . in exchange for services she renders. This much should introduce our point of view."

4. Which came first . . . Love, or Sex?

"There is an excellent rationale for answering this which requires merging several concepts. Polarity has always existed, permitting the balanced in-going and outgoing flows of Life energy. It is also familiar as the Yin-Yang principle. Polarity existed long before human flesh was invented, so that Love existed long before sexual intercourse as humans presently experience it.

"The original flesh Man was hermaphrodite, male and female, complete in one package containing both sexes. Original Man did not procreate except with difficulty, and then only when forced to do so by the Guides of that bygone era. Human sexual intercourse came into being much later, after the division of the sexes. Then note, please, that SEX for humans was/is an afterthought, and will cease to exist to be when human bodies are no longer needed. A date for that End-Time condition has not been given!

"A constant interchange of Life Force, as Love, will always be necessary to keep the Universe moving. Defined as the fundamental creative force of the Universe, Love will always be found flowing where there is human life, but human life also requires more than sex. To have more Life requires More Love, and to perpetuate the race, humans require more sex! A chicken and egg situation, aye?"

5. What is 'Ideal Sex', and what makes it ideal?

"The definition of ideal sex varies widely for different people. It depends on several major factors, presumes excellent health, and includes the state of evolution of mind and soul. If the expectations of both parties are achieved, then perhaps that union is ideal. Speaking technically, any interchange of body currents and fluids between the human male and female which results in a live birth is ideal. Psychically speaking . . . emotionally and spiritually . . . if the purpose was to express a deeper affinity, then *perhaps* the union was ideal. In a higher sense, if true fulfillment is at stake, being One with God, then the feelings and experience of soul union can be said to be ideal only if both parties to the activity were equally well satisfied. If companionship is the end objective of a union between female and male, with an inner peace from sharing Life together, of gratitude for the companionship each with the other, then perhaps THAT is ideal sex for THAT couple. Then SO MUCH depends on the objective for which a union is undertaken, and whether that purpose is consummated."

6. Why am I unable to obtain sexual satisfaction?

"There are several good reasons why the legendary levels of satisfaction from male-female sexual relationships are not always achieved. Perhaps the foremost reason is that a person can only exchange love at the level to which he loves himself. Stated in a psychological vein, if one has low self-esteem, he probably cannot live up to his own aspirations, which surely are to satisfy, to bring perfection to himself and to his or her partner. Perhaps one should investigate the current status of his ADULT-PARENT-CHILD relationships, as used by Berne, to look into what to do about correcting it.

"Resolving emotional and past-life factors belongs more properly to the practicing psychologist and counselor then here. There may also be health problems and physiological factors involved. Perhaps you need an in-depth physical checkup. See also our bibliography. OK?"

7. When Love Fades . . . .

"As seems commonly observed, almost expected, the male libido is highest in a new conquest, and fades rapidly with familiarity. This will nearly always be true when the source of the attraction originates in or is confined 'below the belt,' to the lower chakras. To be exciting enough to be continued for a lifetime with one partner, Humanity needs to find a more challenging and a deeper meaning to the expression of affinity *above* the belt, awakening the higher three chakras. This is true even if limited solely to sexual or tantric intercourse. As described in this text, the quality of sexual love improves as each chakra above the basic gonadal chakra in turn is activated. More or less literally, when the seventh chakra in each human partner is activated, one experiences the Seventh Heaven. Then to experience LOVE beyond mere flesh satiation, satisfying as that can be, one must learn to recognize his and her subtler feelings, as to where they originate, and then how to enhance them, improving their quality and quantity. One also must learn about improving QUALITY, and that TOP QUALITY is accessed only when the top chakras are fully engaged, activated, and used properly, balanced with the lower three chakras. One then may differentiate between which feelings stem from sex and which stem from love. Partners to the sexual processes then can achieve his or her objectives at different levels and still find themselves fulfilled."

8. What about Old Age sex?

"In the space of one lifetime incarnate, it is possible for persons to develop successively higher states of Love, then to remain in a state of Love without needing to use SEX, even to express affinity, mutual respect, or attraction. We claim that sexual intercourse is a convenience, making reproduction attractive, and a very nice convenience to express affinity for persons who can handle its implications. But we say that when sexuality seems unavailable, when a person or couple can no longer make use of it, substitutes better than the original are available, IF DEVELOPED. Sexual intercourse is needed, as in the sense of procreation, only when the higher flows are not activated. Polarity will always exist, as will the potentials for experiencing the sexual current flows. Human sexuality will always exist, but its manner of expression will depend entirely on those who indulge in it."

9. A Closing Comment

"When we find a person or persons maladjusted in their sexual expression, we find a person who has not made a happy adjustment to Life. But attempting to pursue happiness only through the gonads and drugs is unlikely to produce lasting satisfaction, and almost sure to produce serious deterioration of body health, and of said souls as spiritual entities. The effects will be experienced mentally, intuitively, and physically perhaps for aeons yet to come."

2

Are You Having Fun?

"What is FUN to YOU?

"Has it become a drudge to go through the same old effort at getting a belly full of food and booze, then to sleep it off and get a headache or hangover? Is it really satisfying to do the bumps and grinds, in hope of having a few high moments, or maybe a small orgasm?

"Our purpose for doing all this work is to awaken people like you to an unusual opportunity to have REAL fun, but it requires you to clean up your total self and relationships, physiologically, psychologically and spiritually speaking. Wonderful rewards can be yours, even during this incarnation, long before your final curtain is drawn. We offer specific help to Seekers of a better life. For following through rigorously, anyone can become consciously a co-worker through the veil, finding a sense of fulfillment presently unknown to Earthlings.

"We open windows, airing what we mean by 'cleaning up one's case,' and discuss the accelerating changes capable of being experienced by Humanity the world over. We fill in with background appropriate to integrating our pearls into a simple program of education in matters of a deeply philosophical and yet utilitarian nature.

"We refresh you on who YOU are and on who WE are, how we will work together, and why we believe it is important to do the best you can with your time and resources for the next twenty years or so. Some people need only a simple reordering of personal priorities, but for others it may mean making major changes.

"Our readership is already of above intelligence. Particularly encouraged to receive and enter our ministry are persons like you, who recognize what we are talking about, and who seek that elusive life of spirit that is recognized as FUN . . . as FULFILLING . . . as EXHILARATING . . . and who therefore are *willing* to undertake the personal discipline required to ally themselves with our suggested Life Program.

"Our incarnate background and present location in The Heavens enable us to provide you with an integrated program of soul technologies, built of the best from Ancient and Contemporary Religion and Philosophy, Politics, Science, and Education. We provide you with Holistic methods and Spiritual Technologies not yet fathomed by Earth's 'Establishment'.

"The instructions contained in this tome prepare one for the Spiritual Life by developing skill in perfecting the sexual part of flesh life, mastering all aspects of incarnate life through Tantra Yoga. You will turn old stumbling blocks into stepping stones. If we are even only partially successful in reaching into your mind, your sense of fulfillment will still improve remarkably.

"When followed consistently, our exercises are instrumental in improving the mental health of nations by healing the troubled individuals comprising them. Perhaps we could strengthen our position with biblical references, but many original meanings have become lost or are considered occult. The Ancient Wisdoms are now only dimly visible in the religious experience of conventional churchdom. One could truthfully say that the true Christianity has not yet been tried!

"We hope to have built our case convincingly enough so that we can be of continued assistance to you as you go about gaining release from tribulation, boredom, and reincarnation. We are already very busy among Humanity, and will become more so as our materials are circulated, more lectures delivered, and more questions answered and understood. Guided by our unusually perceptive staff of trained clairvoyants Up Here on This Side, our responsive practitioners from all walks of life on Your Side are being trained to clear you as recruits and candidate co-workers of what baffles most of the present-day help-professionals.

"Right this moment we are restoring and clarifying certain important portions of the Bible messages and Ancient Wisdoms, so that whoever wills to enter the Kingdom of Heaven by perfecting his relationships can trust, initiate and complete the classical trip home to the Father's House.

"Could we offer you more?"

CHANNELER/AUTHOR'S ADDENDUM

Rather than being just another book filled with the usual SPOOK-SPEAK or SEX-SPEAK, however adroit, this volume is a collection of channeled discourses originating from our Elder Brothers, addressed to anyone who reads, for alleviation of difficulties in humanity's most sensitive relationships, those of Love. The "Upstairs" contributors to this book have mastered Earth's Life System. Their messages applied will release Humanity from addiction to Sex, Money, Food, Health, Power . . . all palliatives sought by the unrequited and unenlightened Human Spirit. These insights taken to heart, assure passing the Final Exams of Schoolhouse Earth. Here is counsel on sublimating troublesome aspects of Earth life, while still working and living in Joy and Love . . . HAVING FUN AS YOU GO.

For sincerely putting into practice what is offered in these ego-busting "I" Openers, we assure you a bigger bang out of life than is possible from restricting yourself to the standard social approaches. The name of this game is "TAKE CHARGE OF YOUR LIFE."

If you want some REAL fun, start digging!!

3

Hierarchical Viewpoints on Sexuality

If you want to get immediately to the meat of what we have to offer about sexuality, skip this chapter. For others, it may be interesting to gain insight into how interested The Hierarchy of Elders is regarding us "Little Ones" still in the skin.

"Before we get on with our messages for today, we'd like to fill in a few gaps in your understanding of our insistence and purpose in wanting a Psychic Sex Book published and distributed. You know we do not need the money, nor do you need any more books to read for entertainment. You may already be aware of the fact that we, as your Guides, have risen above the restrictions of the Earthplane. We once were chained by our own activities to the astral planes, to the lower parts of the heavens, as many among you are now. In ancient Atlantean times, when we first learned of methods for releasing the human soul, Life was much the same as yours is today. We married and had families. We had jobs and personal problems, experiencing the trials and tribulations that you still experience on Earth today . . . joy, pain, wars, drought, tornadoes . . . the electrical technologies, manned flight . . . the works.

"Life began to change for us as we applied the same ancient teachings to which we refer and teach frequently in our many messages. By mastering those same teachings, we eventually freed ourselves from the same kinds of addictions and pulls that at present hold you captive to embodiment on Earth. We learned, for example, that enslavement to feelings and emotions, as well as to material things, brought about forces that kept us from entering into the higher realms.

"Once convinced of the truths taught by our Old Masters we studied and worked diligently to achieve freedom from confinement to the Earth planes. We made the conscious decision to follow the paths that lead to the very same heaven which you seek. We obtained that coveted Inner Membership by which we could function in the higher states of consciousness at will. As we continued on that upward path, we discovered those mansions of which Christed Jesus often spoke. We chose to do those "extra" things that would make our further incarnation unnecessary. Even as you shall find, we too found that we could leave the Earth permanently by focusing our attentions and efforts on the things that would assure ourselves of being IN the world but not OF it. We HAVE come back into flesh from time to time to take special advantage of world conditions, and to reinstate certain mathematical and political conditions needed to assure Humanity's upward movement. We then readily recall YOUR problems for so recently having reexperienced them . . . less than a hundred years ago ourselves! You would recognize our names. [Since revealed as William Ewart Gladstone and James Clerk Maxwell].

"After having heard OUR side of the story, we do not quite understand why anyone would want to continue returning to Earth, time after time, unnecessarily. We attribute your attachment to the joys and sorrows of the Earth to lack of knowledge or disbelief of what we have found. Thus, in these discourses, we try offering enough insight so that you too shall free yourselves from unnecessary earthy attachments, including sex!

"In this introductory message, we expect to create enough interest so that you will prepare yourselves for experiencing the highest joys while you are enroute to self-mastery. It is only through our Masters' Love for us, and thus our love for you as our younger Sisters and

Brothers that we present this series, for we could just as well have forgotten you and gone into higher states of being, or to other life systems out in the galaxy.

"Rather than leave behind old friends and associates, we decided long ago to work with them through the veil, to help them from This Side to obtain their own releases from the Earth. Yet, we found how difficult it is, working from this side reaching through the veil into the consciousness of our still incarnate friends, to tell them what each one of them needs to become freed, and to see them follow through and achieve that freedom. It requires the help, the literal example of a special incarnate friend, operating through the veil between Heaven and Earth with us, a friend who will stay with aspirants long enough to see them through their trials and tribulations. Each aspirant has to come to certain personal realizations and learn certain lessons that lead to HIS OWN ultimate release from Earth-flesh and relational attachments.

"We readily hear, see, and know what is in the minds and hearts of incarnate humanity. Thus, we understand clearly what is holding Man back from realizing personal heaven consciousness. Only when we are able to communicate, to inject our guiding thoughts into Man's consciousness enough to cause those principles to be part of one's daily awareness . . . only then can we help them become freed forever. It usually takes a long time to bring about individual resurrection from 'spiritual death' into the true life of spirit which we enjoy.

"We have decided to write this book to expand our efforts by giving to those who want to experience conscious reunion with God (and with us) the means and understanding by which they can use Sexuality as one way to attain that glorious freedom, through perfecting themselves in sexual relationships on broader and deeper levels. In short, we think we have found a swift way to release genuine 'Seekers of Truth' from bondage to Earth, if we can show them what is binding them to it. 'To as many as asked, He gave them the power to become Sons of God.' [John 1:12.]

"Now that we have the means to circulate this information among all who are able and willing to read, and to experiment, we expect a much greater response from Humankind than we have seen in the past, than when we had tried working through the Earth's various religious hierarchies. Please note that it is not our intent to attack the churches. Rather, we are seeking to help them by releasing them from the old bonds that have tied *them* to erroneous doctrine through millennia of pagan superstitions and misinterpretations of holy writ.

"The detailed teachings of The Nazarene, and the doctrines that have been handed down through the thousands of years since our victory over flesh, have become largely unrecognizable. Not available in toto in any one document, The Word that *has* survived still contains vestiges of truth. Unfortunately, the more subtle of such truths are visible only to a few people whose interests and studies have shown them how to recognize it, and where it can be found. Then, the Ancient Wisdoms were not kept secret so much as that the usual scholar could not recognize what our documentation could teach them.

"Those subtle truths today are almost never properly interpreted and seldom practiced. Because of intense personal interest and a strong desire for personal release, in the Universities and college courses we conduct up here in 'Angel Institute of Technology [AIT],' dedicated students prepare themselves to be the recipients, practitioners, and in some cases the passers-on of our inspirationally received instructions and guidance as your Prophets, Psychics, Readers, Seers, Channels, and as Teachers.

"As for the churches, we need do little but supplement their works, except where some of their teachers have become antagonistic to those fundamental principles whose practice and acceptance could help people free themselves from their little earth pettinesses and fleshly aggrandizements. We definitely are *not* Fundamentalists in the contemporary religious use of that word!

"You will find surprisingly little of a truly 'sacred' nature in your present scripture except for references toward the kindness and attention of God, and toward Those Prophets who sacrifice their higher privileges and pleasures of Heaven to come down to the Earth, trying to lend relief and guidance to their incarnate fellow creatures.

"We will continue through these discourses, giving our transcriber an opportunity to serve us and you by *showing you how to put our concepts into practice*, by helping you learn how to achieve the quickest and most direct conscious return to the heavens. In this volume and through private therapies which we shall guide to you, we shall stress direct relief from the causes of specific pressing problems affecting your progress.

"Ultimately, through developing your OWN telepathy and intuition, we hope to inspire each of you directly. The Spirit of Truth will then manifest to all persons who accept and undertake the practice of the ideas we set forth in these epistles. Thus, Godspeed to you who aspire to "take the Kingdom of Heaven by storm."

". . . and all this through perfecting one in the processes of Sexuality! It has been done, and still CAN be done."

"Amen!"

CHAPTER

4

Who Wants Psychic *Sex?*

"This book is not about getting laid in a coffin! It *is* offered to persons who find Life dull, who are perhaps sated by unsuccessful or unfulfillable efforts at finding meaning through sex, who are trying to reinject significance into their lives. It is intended to be read by males who are no longer able to maintain an erection, and by females who find it difficult any longer to respond meaningfully to what had previously been a mainstay of physical and subjective delight. More than that, by proposing greater pleasures than have as yet been experienced, this book will surely provide welcomed insight into and relief from what has happened to former straight persons now turned gay, to the lesbians, and to other less venturesome or some straight-minded persons of the world, any or all of whom are unable to find the former happiness or personal and private satisfactions which should be experienced through sexual relations. Some persons will wish to investigate Tantra Yoga more in depth than we have done here. Others will wish to seek and to attain the heights which lie beyond Tantra. We recommend the latter, but can help them all!

"We discuss certain prevailing reasons why there is such widespread dissatisfaction within the world populace. Changing conditions are making Life increasingly difficult to impossible, and continue making it unlikely that persons shall reexperience their former simple pleasures.

"You are probably aware of the encroaching world famine, and have noticed that even in the U.S.A. there is a gradual dearth of good natural food stuffs, of clean water and pure air. Deterioration in each category is becoming sufficiently offensive to damage the responsiveness of the human flesh body and its mind, preventing Spirit from experiencing its fullest capacities in any manner of incarnate expression.

"Indeed, multiple causes for disintegration of human mental and physical performance abound, acting collectively to deaden the higher sensitivities which prevailed among almost all humankind throughout the preceding aeons of Time.

"We are trying to make the point here that the goals of humanity have somehow become of less significance, in that it has become the "in" thing to pursue pleasure above and almost beyond any other form of physical experience, with corresponding diminution and loss of human values. Then, much that formerly made sexual expression of secondary or tertiary value is being lost or superseded by exalting the sexual experience.

"Several important factors have been working silently to undermine the human social value system(s). The severely overpopulated portions of the globe of themselves seem unable to find ways to feed or even to care for themselves. They have nearly lost their incentive, their fundamental energy and capacity to do much of anything constructive for themselves, being minimally able to feed, house and clothe themselves. Only the barest of energies are available to respond to the pressures for self maintenance, and these are usually dissipated sexually.

"We note that Humanity on a large and ever increasing scale is building itself a giant trap, one which is already seen encroaching the borders of those countries where the populace is suffering also from disease and starvation, malnourishment, and loss or lack of goals. Even the U.S.A. is beginning to show signs of having lost its own self-image and WASP or Puritanical traditions of tight strictly-held personal and business ethics.

"Since World War II, the worldwide encroachment of Communism, the diminishing hold of religious institutions over the populace, and the disintegration of our national socio-economic bases for continuing to hold humanity in line with the earlier benevolent despotisms of the world are held largely at blame for the fundamental loss and erosion of personal and national values.

"And where, you ask, does the impetus, the force, come from which is a root-cause of said noted deteriorations? We opine that it originates in lessened fear of or respect for Godliness, and in a widespread and progressive unwillingness to accept personal responsibility, in loss of a sense of self-worth, and for a diminishing lack of effectiveness and loss of respect for those political, religious, and economic forces which formerly perpetuated the old value systems. The shift from a small-town and a family-unit agriculture-based society into a form of impersonal large-scale city living has all but destroyed our sense of community consciousness. An outright lack of practical application of the traditional values of our founding forefathers, however strict, is leading to evisceration of the strong freedom-oriented religious and political system that formerly united society at large.

"In addition to these personal, social and worldwide economic changes, we are seeing significant changes in the world weather patterns, with diminished large-scale food production and distribution. We are seeing emergence of a global transitional political and economic value system superseding former religious values. That not-so-subtle shift is causing individual persons to search for meaning through pleasure, through attempting to build something new and of greater value, to create a satisfying life and world through the act of sexual creativity. Hardly equal to the job already at hand, are ye, aye!

"But . . . you protest . . . why have the values of traditional Judeo-Christendom not been working out? In Man's search for enlightenment, why have the adherents of Christendom themselves not been able to rise above their bounds to slavery in the mental sense, if no longer enslaved in the physical sense? Where has the original spark gone which formal Religion once appeared to supply? And gone indeed it seems to us to be, but there are extenuating circumstances which largely govern the affairs of Humanity overall, forces of which Mankind is yet but little aware. Most peoples of the world have reported generally deteriorating conditions of the planet, or seem to note significant changes. And indeed, there are causes for those changes, some of which we shall now undertake to identify, whether subsequent curative activities are likely to ensue or not.

"Worldwide wars of devastating proportions have taken place, and lesser wars of global attrition continue to be witnessed, partly products of great greed. Instant global awareness of those conflicts hinges largely on worldwide satellite communications, and the fact that some conflicts themselves are fueled by the speedier means of transportation of military and industrial goods from any one point on the globe to almost any other.

"Also, in some societies, entrenched and dissident insurgent groups both are tussling, seeking to disrupt and/or to preserve former tightly-knit ruling societies, formerly isolated by geography and poor communication with the outside world. Human population and economic expansion on a global basis is forcing emergence and integration of new and untried social and religious-economic value systems, is forcing global socio-economic realignment.

"Side effects of the Technological Revolution on the social fiber of the world have become seemingly irreversible and inescapable, but are not being all bad. Some of the changes being wrought are necessary to break up the crystallization of Man and his institutions. However, because the changes have come upon the world so rapidly, in one or two generations, mankind has been caught unprepared. Without having understood the Ancient Wisdoms, it is difficult for Man to adapt from previous Piscean value systems to the New Age Aquarian value system required for personal survival and global harmony. Of immediate concern here is the impact made on the social order by new methods for wide-scale birth control, and by the availability of drugs and alcohol, both so largely damaging to social stability, and being responsible for the explosion of sexual freedom. God is not punishing Man for breaking His laws, Man is breaking *himself* on those laws!

"Consider well that those same Mid-East wars which have erupted are reflecting pressures for rapid change in ages-old social and economic systems. Not limited to the Israelis and Arabs, ancient biblical forces are also operating in the Caucasian and Oriental races. Former Puritan and later WASP values permit only limited sexual and social means of expression. Consider also that the technologies of the 1700's and 1800's could not support widespread interchange of ideas and drugs, restricting dissemination of the knowledge and means for personal debasement and social disintegration.

"Contemporary global transportation and communication of new or different value systems and products is a mixed blessing. While opening up new channels for enlightenment on higher levels, it has also opened new avenues for social intercourse and exploitation of both resources and peoples, economically and politically. The older value systems served well as long as they were unchallenged, and were actually useful in maintaining social order. What formerly was acceptable must now give way to integration of Man on the smaller Planet Earth. Portions of "the old ways" should still be retained, even if perhaps less widely applicable today, because they are still capable of retaining certain key family and group values which ages of previous Life had experienced, had held sacred.

"Centralized Power has always been susceptible to corruption. With the increasing complexity, size, and speed of current governmental and world affairs, it has not been easy to retain individual hold over one's own personal affairs. In the U.S.A. we presently witness the phenomenon that delegation of one's personal prerogatives to Representatives in a remotely located Government, and/or to large benevolently-intended religious or social institutions results in actually relinquishing one's individual birthright of self determination. We are asked to give up personal benefits for a supposedly greater group benefit. This process is being increasingly experienced in Government, Economics, in the Military, in Education and Welfare, and in Religion as a factor to be reckoned with. Add to that the steady loss of arable land and forested areas, changing world weather and rainfall patterns, increased pollution of water and foods resources . . . all are now threatening to assume disastrous proportions in the near-term future. Added together, the inner and the outer pressures for change contribute to a stressful situation for most Earthlings, and hence increase the pressures for pursuit of immediate satisfaction, above and beyond physical means.

"At one time in these United States of America it was the normal pattern of living for most small-town people to have a small farm or plot of Earth on which to grow the majority of one's own fruits, vegetables, grains and dairy products in addition to one's trade or profession.

"As we enter the year 2000, now, with city-states, the population explosion and shifting personal value systems, it has become essentially impossible for most persons to be independent, to plan ahead, to delay immediate gratification of wants for enjoyment in a later and certain future. It was possible, when the generously endowed and slightly populated remote portions of the world were still available as frontiers, that a man and his family could upset their former established patterns of living and go re-establish themselves in a new territory. The pattern was then to exploit the new area, to mine it, until it too became unable to produce or to provide the original support and surpluses. That process led to invention of fertilizers and crop rotation, which then and now enable a few to feed vast numbers of city dwellers.

"In other words, the shift from an agrarian society to a technological society has accelerated shifts in worldwide population and its value systems, causing displacement of social patterns, and indeed having nearly outlawed what had long been held sacrosanct as The Only Way to Live. Then identifying them as "the good old days" in early America does not hide certain former difficulties in eking out life from difficult straits. Lack of cheap power and large scale transportation on today's scale contributed greatly to shortages of fuel and food even then. Exploitation of undeveloped relatively unlimited free energy resources was not considered as a significant factor just as long as there were trees to fell for fuel and timber to saw up for housing.

"Consider today the plight in which unrestricted burning and slashing of Central American rain forests has denuded vast areas now unfit for agricultural life. International ecosystems experts recognize that loss of those precious rain forests is halving the world's oxygen-producing greenery, with unpredictable consequences. Consider as well the effects that such rapine practices as cutting and burning have on the world's Animal and Biological Kingdoms, and upsetting the

Food Chains of the world.

"Contributing also to the major upsetting of world conditions have been large uncontrolled forest fires, and the man-made destruction of land resources caused by strip mining the Earth's surface of resources and vitality which by and large are unlikely ever to be replenished, generating new Sahara Deserts, even if not entirely realized within the life span of those who will be reading this documentary.

"Where does all this lead? And of what useful significance is it all, whether true or not, to enhancement of the implied theme of SPIRITUALIZING SEXUALITY? There is indeed a connection through a network of intertwining events, each and all factors contributing to the present worldwide change in values. Mankind had indeed become crystallized on quasi-Piscean values, so that changes are inevitable to ushering in the Aquarian Age, as we deem it.

"However else we might choose to label the contributing factors, we still have yet to consider the effects that Human Mind Technology may yet make possible in reducing the globally disastrous effects of contemporary war-making or defense thinking on energy and resource expenditures for destruction and war-making capability.

"One serious flaw in national thinking lies in continued diversion of high-minded technologists and technologies from food production and life-improving applications, permitting exploitation and destruction of wide areas of prime arable land for residential and industrial purposes. Expanded emphasis on building war-making machinery subtly erodes our human value systems, posing near-term destruction of social and economic systems which at one time produced food supplies large enough to feed a major portion of the globe. Diversity in food production is sacrificed as vast areas become nonproductive by covering the most productive lands with parking lots and buildings. Man could easily erect his communities on nonproductive land or on the hillsides.

"Individual greed, and lust for POWER and CONTROL triumph, with the world-at-large being much the loser. One result invisible to incarnate Humanity is that Earth's problems are backing up into the Life Behind The Veil, causing Hierarchical intervention, as at present, with initiation of those great changes which are assuring the Aquarian

Age of its timely arrival.

"All of this stems from and is generated by short-sighted misuse of the Human Mind. Whatever Man focuses his collective mind on comes to pass. Then the blame for our present conditions lies not on only a few highly placed persons, but lies squarely on the entire masses of humanity. The ministry of Mass-Media Communications has only speeded up the process. Those same beneficent communications agencies which make handsome profits from using a natural resource (radio waves) by selling doom and antihumanitarian viewpoints and unrest, *could* unite the world with their propangandizing capacities. That portion of the Human Experience which is of good report is consistently down-played and ignored in favor of the differences and out-of-place negativism. Loss of heart, loss of face, loss of hope, and lack of belief in the ultimate goodness of Humanity are seriously undermining what should be the norm.

"The bottom line for all this in the U.S.A. has been to "make a fast buck," sacrificing long-term gain for temporary advantage. For perhaps six generations the U.S.A. has been viewed, even by the more despotic-seeming agencies of World Religion and Economics, as the jewel of planet Earth. In effect, those same forces of expediency are creating the loss of human values by which the U.S.A. is losing its reputation and luster.

"And yet, for all its turmoils, the U.S.A. is still probably the best of all places still available to live. Through recognizing what values should be placed first, we may have time enough to reverse our fall.

"While all of the above items in one or more ways contribute to the demise of our present form of civilization, another factor is not yet recognized by those humans who would lead us. As seen from On High, a predictable consequence is that the peoples of planet Earth will pay dearly through loss of opportunity for reincarnating soon, for easily experiencing Earth as a gentle jewel in the heavens. Not until Earth has again been restored can the normal Schoolhouse be so available on Earth. The waiting lines will be several thousands of years long, until we again have a cleansed planetary surface and atmosphere, and an Aquarian Age outlook on Life and its purposes.

"Then perhaps the key word in all this has been EXPLOITATION of one human by another, or of one group by another. We assure you that the central theme of this book is about PROPER use of the Creative Life Force rather than about misapplication of the very Creative Process itself. We might coin the word "sexploitation." We shall be discoursing on the various factors inherent in personal use of the Creative Life Force, how it can be experienced even while developing greater capacity for life in the higher levels. We shall also discourse on what is likely to be experienced by the unwary, and shall offer a route to recovery of Self Respect by going on beyond Sexuality for those persons who have not entirely lost hope of recovering their feelings of accomplishment and personal fulfillment in their present incarnations.

"Ours is indeed a high goal, a most satisfying goal, reachable through a balanced use of sex and the human mind in higher levels than have been taught widely. We offer several processes by which YOU can make available those higher forces in your own life.

Read on please, dear reader, READ ON!"

A PEEK AHEAD

"Labor that formerly produced robust physical health is now seldom seen over wide portions of the globe, so it is not surprising that creeping body-mind debilitation abounds, to the detriment and gradual inability of a person to maintain health good enough to retain his innate physical and spiritual functions.

"Consider the declining birthrate in the higher income and the middle-class intellectual communities. Entire lives are now spent in the cities and factories in foul-smelling airs. Our foods are grown on foreign soil, or in fields filled with pesticides. Creativity is dulled through the sheer mental drudgery of production line economy. Pride in personal accomplishment is becoming a rare thing. Vicarious living through the lives of our television heroes occupies such a large part of our sedentary activity that our bodies and minds are unchallenged, and thus deteriorate, and we do not even seem to care! The simple life has been forgotten in the rush to obtain things, prestige, and power. Even the capacity to enjoy simple things like our human sexuality has largely been lost by an artificial value system become topsy-turvy.

"The time has now come when young people, people in their thirties and forties, now experience certain processes formerly observed only in elderly males: the penis bends and the knees do not!

"The struggle for equality between the male and the female halves of the world also has upset patterns by which a workable arrangement had been achieved in previous social and business worlds. The Equal Rights people indeed have some good points, but many persons, both male AND female, continue to be exploited. When the Equal Rights Movement reverted to militant feminists who have lost their own unhinged mental points of view, they further unbalanced the forward-moving forces of the universe.

"Any vociferant person or group which today has not been overcome by or succumbed to "The System" is able to triumph over a clear majority of complacent persons who may or may not be well-adjusted. The trend to faction-ridden societies like we experience today is stirred because so many complacent persons are unwilling or afraid to fight the status quo. Disquieted persons find allies of many unlikely sorts, pooling their resources to tear down values that have persisted through time, thereby making a tragedy for the well-adjusted and usually well positioned person.

"In other words, some dissident minority persons are today minded to wrest control from the disorganized non-militant majority while seeking to get its satisfactions, not through becoming well adjusted to life, but to make the world conform to ITS value systems. Too often we find that such special interest groups have unreasonable personal goals which run counter to the benefits and interests of the greater common good. We refer to and include some the church and social institutions of the world.

"A major problem for the Humanity of today is to gain control over its own welfare. In the United States of America this amounts to the government once again being controlled BY the people FOR the people, instead of being pressured into submission by special and limited interests. Institutions out of control include the Military, the Religions, Education, Big Business, and Big Government itself.

"Seemingly lost in the shuffle is the god-given true inner sense of human values, from which personality values stem, those values which are of an Eternal Nature and should underlie our societal mores and traditions, like the Judeo-Christian ethic did for the Piscean Age.

"Our persistent thesis is preservation of certain *personal* values which go beyond what has become inculcated in the U.S.A. socio-political system, and this by way of reestablishing the connection between one's innate Spirituality and Sexuality. The individual and God ARE One, whether fully sensed or not. The element of PER-SONAL RESPONSIBILITY then becomes paramount. Pursuit of that realization by all humans on the planet as we offer here will surely bring about restoration of Edenic conditions, if they are ever again restored here on the planet Earth in a finite passage of Time.

"How do we start? By examining more closely that mystical quality the world is seeking. As sung so eloquently, 'Ah, 'tis Love and Love alone the world is seeking . . .' Yes, the REAL THING!

"And it all begins with Thee and Me!"

CHAPTER

5

The Real Thing

In the classics of literature, TRUE LOVE is usually focused and experienced on the level of personality. It has the ingredients of good looks, sex appeal or lust, perhaps shared interests, and on some felt need satisfied. A more perfect love may still include personal factors, but enlarges into unconditional, impersonal . . . or *trans*personal love. Please note that we did not say UN-personal or depersonalized love, but a more expanded SOUL love . . . a truly *spiritual* affinity on the deepest levels . . . on all levels. Fortunately, a person can expand his or her consciousness to experience, understand and manifest that newer and higher quality of Love.

"To explain how this is done is not an easy thing to complete all in one session, but we shall all be richer for the attempt. Therefore, be prepared to devote undivided attention to our offering this morning.

"Unless you are a good actor, it is not at all unusual to find yourself unable to muster emotional pangs at will. Emotions are often rooted in energy patterns which do not necessarily relate to true or impersonal Love as WE define it. Instead, the emotional aspect of said quality may derive from threatened or actual feelings of loss, of deprivation of a cherished object, whether personal or objectified in some material substance. When we next find time or opportunity to engage you more deeply into the more profound insights, as to the more occult aspects of genuinely defined LOVE, in its fullest sense, we shall take advantage of you to ask you to set aside time for relaxed receptivity. We trust then not to find you at all resenting the seeming intrusion of our offerings, but shall tend that way, in that manner, to find you both willing and able to undertake further in-depth researches into what WE mean when WE use the cognomen IMPERSONAL LOVE.

"Real Love . . . Impersonal Love . . . will be found to be a Force, having NO LIMITS to its expansion. It makes no demands and forges no bonds on the resources or attention of another person, then giving total freedom to each and to both parties to come or to go at will, and to engage in a similar relationship with other humans. For once having cognized the existence of a greater love, it may be recalled that what has almost always been CALLED Love falls short indeed of the deeper meanings, feelings and content of the true Impersonal or Unconditional Love.

"Consider it potentially a sign of genuine love when one person can, in spirit, permit another to enter and to leave a relationship entirely at his or her own convenience. However, on the human personality level of commitment, this does not at all encourage or mean avoiding mutually assumed family or business responsibilities. Real Love includes honoring one's commitments and combining personal resources to fulfill a contracted relationship. The freedom to be one's self does require that a person be allowed to explore and to do what he or she finds necessary without tying down a mate or companion unfairly or irresponsibly.

"When a person is haunted by memories of some past affair or flirtation, as when recalling the feelings of unrestricted total acceptance, it is well to identify those feelings as being typical of the sort of Love of which we address, of the sort where there are no strings on any level. That true sense can be continued, preserved as long as one lives, and even beyond death of the physical senses. In the truest sense, these evidences are typical of the finer more readily accepted and visualized forms of the impersonal love manifested by The Masters. Still manifesting through Personality, through Personage, they still are nevertheless appropriate to general Mankind.

"With the advancement of human evolution, eventually each incarnate Earthling will develop, manifest and share that high sort of affinity. The rapport of Impersonal or True Love can and surely shall survive and transcend personal love, and will outlaw and totally eliminate jealousy. Note, please, that jealousy implies strong and deep feelings of inadequacy, and perhaps a sense of OWNERSHIP, neither being proper elements of True Love. Retention of such personal traits results in an unworthiness and an inability to experience True Love.

"We are making the necessary effort in polishing up our definition of Impersonal Love so that you will recognize enough of its characteristics to know what to focus your attention on. As with nearly all abstract concepts, it is difficult to define enough of the qualities which necessarily pervade and persist in all levels of Love to be both recognizable and then be implemented. We believe that what has already been given, if sincerely taken to heart, would satisfactorily explain where upon the classical definitions of love falter and fail.

"To develop a sense of Impersonal Love requires little else than persistent attention to polish one's personality. This is most effectively and rapidly done by observing your own personal thoughts and feelings and the effect your *own* thoughts and feelings have on your *associates*, and vice versa.

"Perhaps we have been successful in telling you, in teaching you, that by learning to perceive in the realms of Feeling and Abstract Thought that you will become clairvoyant enough to be at cause-point in all human relationships and thus become a Master of Love. Sort out the different aspects of these definitions, then to list them more carefully for subsequent study and application.

"We cannot go much further in defining intellectually the principles involved than we already have, but since Love and Sexuality are still muchly debated topics there on the planet, let us make a more serious try at satisfying unresolved human emotional needs, providing something more to discuss, to belabor, and debate. Then, when your next opportunity arrives for class discussion, for delivering a sermon, or expounding on some previously-given hierarchical position, or to research for yourself, you will not lack useful materials.

"At the outset it usually makes little difference where you start when trying to glean and/or offer clearer or more efficient definitions of what Love is all about, since there are SO FEW people who care to understand from whence their deeper feelings of either lust or appreciation stem. When we DO occasionally discover someone who REALLY WANTS TO KNOW, and enlists Our help to guide them, it becomes almost a chore for us to have to review the older written word, then to re-frame the findings in such terms that said occasional Student-of-Life is able to sate himself. We then encourage the serious Student of Love to undertake his or her own exhaustive researches in related writings, perhaps starting from the bibliography of this book: surely one source will lead to or suggest another. Then learning further application of the principles will result in attaining even yet a deeper feeling or appreciation for already-observed affinities.

"For discovering the psychological tie-ins between the Mind, Love and The Emotions, for once having gained meaningful interpretations, you will more or less stumble into discovery of what it is that merits further study and development on your own case. A further effort at expansion of one's sense of appreciation for finding and clearing one's blocks and protective programming will be well rewarded, making worthwhile our further efforts at channeling to upgrade your particular Earth-experience of Love. Fulfilled Impersonal Love while incarnate is still much less understood, and hence much less experienced than it need be.

"For having so long discerned and now reported said lack of understanding of Love, having witnessed SO MUCH DISTRESS where there should or COULD be more of the genuine article of Love, perhaps we should rejoice at having found a Channel and a Reader through whom we can work. You have once more made it possible to broadcast further the more fitting, the more accurate and uplifting definitions. For having once again released insight and access into the finer dimensions, perhaps we should do more to help certain responsive persons in their OWN search for overall higher levels of appreciation, then again slowly but certainly helping to spread the Wisdoms and Knowledge and FEELING of genuine love. Even as such gains are made, it becomes more and more possible for still others incarnate upon the Earth to enjoy the truer fruits of personal affinities and mutual appreciations to be explored and experienced. Then for having done this much, we are enabled again to witness greater demonstrations more frequently made possible, augmenting the efforts of those who would make anything at all perfect in their personal incarnations.

"Today marks the resumption of our formal efforts at offering expanded points of view on Love. As insight is gained into the deeper aspects of Love as existing entirely outside of and above Sexuality, perhaps certain few persons will more carefully explore their casual sexual expression, that it might be expressed under conditions where a genuine PRODUCT of Love is anticipated. In other words, where there is a greater and a higher RECOGNITION of the Love expression, plus a deeper understanding regarding the PROCESSES of exchanging the experience of Love, there would be much less NEED of expressed sexuality, with great benefit to the overall spiritual and tangible welfare of the entire planet. In that manner we introduce a bridge between Sexuality and Spirituality.

"If Impersonal Love were widely experienced, the planet Earth as a working entity participating in the overall Galactic Life Plan would be populated with perhaps one tenth so many personages. As one result, incarnate life would be found much more readily adapted to living conditions favoring the restoration, expansion, and the perfection of fully spiritualized Life, along with preservation of sexual love. There would also be noted vastly less of the conditions of general strife, for the conditions on the planet would permit maintenance of pure conditions of sky and soul, water and fuel, of field and forest, such that nearly ALL formerly-seen forms of Life could once again coexist, with no need for loss of entire Life Waves as we now witness.

"In other words, were it more readily possible for one to learn and thus to KNOW of the sources of his or her presently-experienced feelings, whether of RUT and LUST or of AFFINITY and LOVE, a person would surely then act in accordance with same. Efforts at expressing feelings of Love on the physical level are then greatly overworked, in the sense WE see them continuing to be expressed or exploited. Once said TRUE definitions and understanding are gained, it would then be *feasible* to restore the near-idyllic conditions which indeed prevailed in certain earlier visitations of advanced forms of human life on the planet Earth. (See the URANTIA Book)

"Seldom recognized is the fact that Earth's earlier conditions of simplicity and purity actually fostered the development and evolution of the higher forms and levels of life expression. Indeed, during those prehistoric times, earlier forms of life were being tested to determine which were suited for human occupancy, so that setting up conditions of living and reproducing the nascent human forms took precedence over the immediate experience of Love and the finer essences of Mind-Life. It was found, as soon as the human life forms gained supremacy over the lower forms and of their own necessary procreative processes, that there were those adventuresome nascent human souls which counted themselves as having been given total free rein to experience ANYTHING they wanted to try while incarnate. Having been given free will and the overall limited means and conditions of expression which then indeed prevailed, we were hardly able to deny them their whim, without regard for the consequences.

"Then TRUE LOVE as is presently being defined and reviewed here was then indeed seldom experienced, and then only rarely or occasionally by those Higher Beings who were guiding development of the human vehicles, and indeed recognized that inceptive quality. Sexuality as the new and unique means for reproduction became the sole method available to express mutual affinities, and even then it had to be spiced up with intense feelings of joy before sexual reproduction became well established. Few enough indeed were the available means of gratification to the earlier forms of incarnate human embodiment to attract candidates.

"Then, whatever other forms of actual pleasure were found, the development of sexuality was certainly favored by the Ancient Hierarchy, in view of the overall requirement to populate an entire planet as a place to evolve the Human Race. Even then, it was necessary to generate a desire strong enough so that the fledgling Earthlings of that era would undergo the inconvenience to copulate. To this day, to replicate physical forms for expressing Life, feelings strong and prevalent enough to do the task of populating a planet persist. Indeed, in some quarters it may be considered that reproduction is out of control.

"Perhaps we could help you to understand why other forms of

expression were not developed, why We of The Hierarchy did not build other means or qualities such as Affinity and Appreciation, of Love, into Man in its higher experiential levels at that time. Quite simply, the germ of Mind had not yet been developed that far. When we stand back and attempt looking over what Man has been doing with its relatively unrestricted freedom of expression of the reproductive energies and his still nascent Mind, except for his relatively minor technological advance, we readily understand why there are still many souls who seek opportunity to incarnate and express an amply rewarding life. Not being well enough advanced in Spirit, they cannot find as much of interest to do Above as they can find in Earthlife, to the point where conditions within the human soul are really little different than they were many millions of years ago.

"Too many human spirits are seeking opportunity to EXPLOIT SEXUALITY, to continue manifesting their FEELINGS of LUST. Now that the world is overpopulated, they continue their lusts without regard for and while deliberately avoiding the original purpose of sexual expression. FAR TOO FEW humans today are found equipped at the higher levels of Mind to be experiencing enough of TRUE or IMPERSONAL LOVE. One result is that upward evolution of the human SPIRIT as HUMAN SOUL has essentially stalemated, has in fact already so slowed down so much as to be a real problem for The Hierarchy. In the current planetary housecleaning which is today being experienced, said Hierarchy wants to find those few souls which are ABLE as well as WILLING to love as originally intended, and go on to higher levels of Life with Them. Our Channeler-Author's recruiting and training activities reflect Our aims at remedying that situation!

"We are, then, carefully focussing this (morning's) discourse on what Unconditional Love is and is not, so that further private and/or personal investigation and study will be undertaken, so that the evanescence of True Love can be sampled, sensed, becoming more readily and more greatly appreciated, not to mention becoming more widely practiced and experienced. For having gained a higher truer sense of Impersonal Love, we shall observe more of what was originally intended as Galaxy-wide Appreciation of one form of Life for another, with the immediate result that the phenomena and presence of Earth's wars and pestilence need never again be experienced. Lack and disease will become a thing of the past when there are no longer those personal unbalances which allow generation of unfavorable thought forms, then being rid of their sources of creation.

"We are saying here that once the human mind became poisoned and hence insensitive to these higher forms of expressing Love, Acceptance, and Affinity, even the old favored wisdom of just enjoying the continuing presence and humanness of Life in flesh became jaded. Until that condition is righted, Human life can hardly again flourish.

"By whatever means accomplished, when Sexuality and Spirituality are merged, the seeming NEED for exploitation of attractiveness of male—female, expressed through use of the gonadal devices will simply vanish. Not that there cannot ever again be found the conveniences of having another oppositely-sexed body around to delightfully discharge one's built-up tensions and pressures, but those same old sensuality feelings will be secondary to other forms of expression. They will simply not arise unless there IS INDEED the DESIRE of SPIRIT to replicate, to reproduce in the deliberate and planned effort to provide an entry into Materiality through provision of flesh bodies, again REGARDLESS OF THE INCONVENIENCE THEREOF to the parties concerned.

"Take it from us when we suggest that today's world-favorite form for expression of affinity is both that of Convenience and Ignorance in expressing a passion at body-level, and hardly ever is it a case of expressing the more subtle higher affinities.

"NOW, let it be understood that it is indeed possible and often noted that simultaneous expression of true attraction and lust take place. The Grand Plan asks only that human sperm meet a human egg, and leaves all the other details of the life to follow to the participants. In fact, when there is a pregnancy resulting, it usually results from some mix of both pressures, when not done in outright rape conditions . . . whether said rape takes place under matrimonial conditions or through casual sexual brutality.

"Far and away too many persons undertake the lower levels of sexual expression for lack of having anything at all in their lives which is of a satisfying creative nature. When people have not developed suitable release for their inner or spiritual creative pressures, all they are able to recognize and respond to is the usual sexual route to relief. We would surely opt for the inhabitants of planet Earth to undertake study of the higher forms of Creativity. Available are the fields of Design, Music, Art, Sculpture, Invention, Mathematics, Politics, Economics, Philosophy, the Metaphysical arts and sciences, most all in some expression requiring the higher or more abstract mental-spiritual pursuits, seeing then to the elevation of planetary conditions of both body and mind/soul.

"Too few have been the times when Mankind had generated a Golden Age, a Golden Era, in which it was possible for the very highest of incarnate souls to leave a heritage of which subsequent ages and generations could be at once proud, understand, and serve as examples of what Human Life COULD be like for them.

"We wind down this exposition on Unconditional or Impersonal Love by suggesting that what we are seeing overall on the planet and yet individually is the sure collective result of one's individual attitudes and outlook on what True Love is. What a person holds as his or her definition of Love then guides them through expression of that feeling in each and all of their interhuman interrelationships. It is important then, that we shall do all WE can do to help sensitive and upward-seeking persons/souls to bring their own definition and practices of Love more in total conformance to the Hierarchically-intended definition and expression of Love. Yes, what the world is dying for is LOVE . . . the REAL THING! Then Practice what you can learn, separating what leads to GREATER LOVE WHILE INCARNATE, leaving behind that which can seem or become sordid. Sexuality is then hardly more than a normal part of the Real Thing. Do you see it yet? We hope so and will apply ourselves to later additional writings as seen needed, and wanted.

"Let us append some ideas and terminologies that will help us further in expounding more deeply on what are considered to be additional elements of expressed Love. Let LOVE be taken as an aggregation of ideas, concepts, and even as necessary ways to enable you to consider yourself as either being *with* Love or *without* it. We do not say being IN Love, but being WITH Love.

"Love is then a caring for the welfare of and enhancing the Peace within a companion. Love can then be taken as CARING for and ministering to another's State of Mind, doing what appears to be necessary to help that aching other person work through his or her condition of unlovedness. By following through with constructive insights, verbal consolation, of caring enough to be a temporary crutch for one who is emotionally unable to care for himself, one surely finds a warm place in the psyche of said ailing friend.

"We do not adduce that True Love necessitates picking up all the bills of another person until said ailing person is again willing and/or able to carry forward on his or her own steam. We DO mean to help with generation and materialization of the IDEAS, the THOUGHT FORMS of well-being. When a person becomes able again to manipulate the Energy of Thought on his own behalf in the proper manner, it is then a foregone conclusion that he or she can handle ANYTHING ELSE in said Life.

"Then expressing True Love means, in part, the ability to HELP ANOTHER PERSON or SOUL to regain complete control over himself, his thoughts, and hence of his inner feeling conditions . . . and then automatically being in control over his OUTER manifestations. Then we do not include expression of Love to mean doing FOR a person what he or she is perfectly capable of doing FOR HIMSELF. THAT becomes INDULGENCE, often leads to slavery to hypochondriacal personality, and is not Love.

"Then one cannot use or withhold Love as a bargaining chip, tool, or as a crutch, cannot become dependent upon the largess of another human soul, without losing any vestiges of Love. Sometimes it will be found that genuine-article Love will require that one person seem momentarily to abandon another, until the said needy person learns to do FOR HIMSELF what is normal and natural. One's personal evolutionary state then merits consideration of the actualities of a situation, before exhausting one's resources in helping another person.

"One should consider the point of view that human SOUL GROWTH is more important than is human Personality development. A would-be helper or therapist/counselor must handily identify whether the need originates on the SOUL level, or whether it originates in the lower ego or Personality aspect. Let the would-be helper discern and minister to the *real* need.

"As when training children, sometimes the greatest kindness is to help an ailing person confront what only HE or SHE can and/or must confront. Called "loving tough," setting up a person to solve a particular personal problem is then sometimes requisite of True Love, contrasting greatly to DOING SOMETHING *FOR* said person. The factors surrounding the situation dictate the considerations implemented; how they are met then becomes all important.

"A normal portion of expressing Unconditional Love is to be SUPPORTIVE of a person as a way to help them over or through a morass. It should readily be seen that to do one's homework FOR a person is foolish, often nonconstructive, and hence not at all a true kindness or an act of Love.

"Then appropriate care taken as to the manner of expressing Affinity and Appreciation includes the kind word, a hug or perhaps even a respectful touch. These can transmit inner feelings of tender rapport and support, of appreciation even for the Presence of another person in fact or in thought. BEING AVAILABLE, APPROACH-ABLE, is then a large portion of the fact of EXPRESSED Love of the Unconditional variety, and hence need not at all be limited to opposite sexes. Then if there be a great error, it is in misuse, inappropriate personal use, of one's expression of affinity.

"See?"

CHAPTER

6

On Having One's Cake . . .

"Has it occurred to you that there is a fundamental process in living that applies to more or less anything we humans might dream up to do? Like eating the proverbial piece of cake . . . when we do it is gone forever. Yet if we do not eat it, either somebody else will, or it will crumble away, also then to become lost to us forever.

"Similar things happen in life, between females and males. Haven't you occasionally seen some gorgeous frame, with all the right curves and ripples of flesh, gazing at you with an intent and deep interest, like wanting to know you better?

"Or have you had the situation where you were already more or less satiated, and yet, there goes another attractive target of opportunity . . . but you cannot do anything about it, being presently committed, or are otherwise unable to enjoy the promise of a delightful interlude.

"We are sure you have heard the phrase "the grass is always greener on the other side of the fence." Not limited to people, aye, the phenomenon seems to inflict air-breathing mammals of all types.

"For a moment presume that you are reasonably happily married, and that a vision of loveliness parades before you, perhaps innocently at first, and you cannot help but be smitten. Perhaps there is a deja vu, an impulse to arrange an introduction. All these things are normal, but WHAT IS A PERSON TO DO to STAY OUT OF TROUBLE . . . or at least be spared the expense, the embarrassment and inconvenience of a liaison?

"Where do Fate and Common Sense fit in here?

"If you politely decline, will you likely miss anything for All Time?

"When it comes to paying the piper, WHO or what IS the piper?

"There must be some way to communicate affinity without becoming entrapped in a situation that is not conducive to maintenance of domestic tranquility, to let the other party recognize and be recognized. There IS SUCH A WAY, but it is not often used, is seldom ever heard of, and is not at all easy to practice. Yet, for practicing it, the greatest ability for expressing love *ever* will become yours forevermore.

"We speak of developing IMPERSONAL LOVE, transpersonal love, love of the sort exhibited by Jesus of Nazareth and by a few of today's saints still incarnate, perhaps typified by Sathya Sai Baba. To take advantage of what *is* and what *can* be known about transpersonal love requires a high level of dedication, and being honest with one's inner self like nothing you have yet had to practice.

"Now that we have introduced ourselves as being interested in assisting our incarnate younger brethren to be happy though married, perhaps we can spend some of your reading time looking more in depth at the social structures in which we as humans have had to function, essentially from the very Beginning. It has not always made sense that God should have given Man such a wonderful and powerful gift as the power to create, to reproduce himself, and then to tell him that he should not use it for pleasure.

"One of the chief pieces of evidence we can offer for restricting the reproductive function is that in several portions of the globe, the population has outstripped its capacity for supporting its own progeny. Another example problem is the extent to which the lesser developed persons/souls/races appear to procreate without thought for its progeny. Added to that, the federal government of the USA and various state governments as well encourage illegitimacy through paying for unwed mother and child support, without demanding sterilization or other cessation of the supposed 'right' to procreate at random.

"It is viewed up here as some sort of travesty on Justice that the humans most able to take care of their offspring are the least likely to produce children. Something IS INDEED out of whack!

"One learns relatively soon after beginning to study the contemporary world sociological scene that there is indeed little correlation between sexual activity and love, per se. However, in that small correlation coefficient is enough impetus to allow participants still 'on the fence' to agree to succumb to that most powerful of interpersonal events we shall identify as copulation, with or without hope of orgasm.

"NOW, were it only considered 'macho' to boast of one's sexual conquest of the other sex, that would perhaps be enough to justify what we continually see. But WE see evidence that being considered 'macho' increasingly among the lower economic strata means to prove virility through impregnating some female, and the more conquests, the greater is the charm or 'macho' assessment.

"Even before that level of male has proved his virility, he usually forgets who he impregnated and goes off to the next potential victim or customer, without a shred of care for responsibility entering his head.

"Now . . . it can perhaps be more readily accepted as to how this situation has become so overwhelmingly evident these past fifty years when we review the relatively high levels of employment and easy living in the USA during and immediately after WW II, and the corresponding droughts and famines among third world nations. It seems, and correctly so, that there was and still is a HUGE backlog of human souls who will now take almost ANY opportunity to return into incarnation while times are so good. If they do not take their chances NOW, they will probably have to wait in limbo several more thousands of years, until world economic conditions again favor or permit reincarnation in good times.

"We then are witnessing an unusual instance of the urgency to express life being so great that the lesser-developed minds, the psychic or unreasoning minds, are susceptible to pressures from subtle sources to "get in the game and give it the old college try."

"The System, as it is convenient for us to label it, is self-adjusting. While there is a social trauma on the part of the persons most influenced and effected by their own sexual hyperactivity, the middle-classes will for awhile, have to pick up the tab. As the middle-class population dwindles, like it always does recurrently in two-thousand-year cycles, soon again there will be only the extremely poor, and the wealthy.

"Let it be recognized that the middle-class personages, with occasional exceptions for special cosmic reasons, is that class of personages most likely to observe and to heed the God-given rules for living life, so that the goal of individual christing is most often pursued. Then it is not at all necessarily true that the upper-class is more spiritually oriented or adept than the middle classes, nor more so than the lower classes. But it turns out that persons who do not NEED nor particularly DESIRE wealth, are those who have both the time and the inclination to find out what makes Life worthwhile, and then to seek it out and fulfill it.

"We then today address ourselves to those persons most likely to read this sort of material, and who, for having done so, are also most likely to study, evaluate, and elect to live their lives accordingly for their own greatest personal spiritual payoff, whether said payoff is in this or a later lifetime, through a few special parallel relationships, or in the overall sense of graduating from Ye Olde Schoolhouse Earth.

"Let us then consider some of the factors which make it either easy or difficult for a typical Earthling to rise above the call of his or her gonads, and at the same time, to direct said Life currents into the proper channels for realizing the highest good of which he or she is capable of visualizing.

"The seven-year cycles of growing up as humans are well identified. Said cycles make it rather convenient to be able to classify a person and his or her troubles by the age group in which they fall. It is readily apparent that most persons spend their first 13-18 years in preparing themselves mentally and physically for participation in the affairs of the world. A few go on to higher levels of specialized education, but seldom do the members of any age group fail to experience the problems common to those categories of body age.

"When a person in suburban USA reaches the nominal age of 21 he or she is allowed to drink alcohol, is awarded the keys to a car, takes employment, and henceforth tries to live up to his or her goals, or to the goals his social circles enforce on him. However it may appear, his social mores are by then already preestablished through his or her family relationships and with his more general associates up until that time. From that time forward, most persons do not again undertake to improve their ability to confront life until some urgency forces them to do so.

"In other words, when the pressures for change appear, usually and only then will a human stir himself to be rid of the aches and pains in the social or the physiological world, and then, the usual approach is to relieve the symptoms rather than to remove the cause.

"But back to our theme!

"Simply enough stated, it IS POSSIBLE to eat one's cake and to have it too! One does so by making his cake a part of himself on higher levels than he or she is accustomed. Since the ideal oneness between persons is achieved through merging at higher levels, it follows that you can also become one with ANY PERSON, THING, or SITUATION which you wish to identify closely enough with. It is readily possible to cultivate that capability, as given by the following exercises."

Exercises for Eating Your Cake

I. Practice becoming more aware of your own thoughts and feelings, and of how they control your confrontations with your own body and with your fellow creatures and with Life itself.

Practice being aware of the thoughts and feelings of your associates, and of the effects they have on YOU. You will gradually note that you are able to sense their innermost ruminations, being an open book to you. You will thus be in complete charge of any situation you wish to control. At that time, you will need also develop the wisdom to LET THINGS BE. You are NOT responsible for anything or anyone other than your own performance and beingness. In other words, the name of the game is to Be Aware of your surroundings, but responsible only for your own responses.

In other words, you can effectively use this method for becoming clairvoyant at your earliest time, and in the safest manner, naturally.

II. Select an object, perhaps an ashtray or a doorknob, and focus your attention on it. Carefully and slowly learn to perceive its temperature and your feelings toward it. Perceive its texture, its colors, its weight. Look at its surface, to see if it is smooth, roughened, shiny, fuzzy, if it has any shape to it at all. Learn to USE ALL of your present perceptive devices.

While doing these exercises, learn to sense whether you LIKE the object. See if you have ANY FEELINGS toward it. Does the object like YOU? To the extent that you can do so, learn to probe mentally into said object, to merge your consciousness with it. When first doing this it is often easier to begin with a plant than with an inanimate object, something having sentient life, a growing or potted plant being preferred to a clipped stem of a plant. Eventually, you will find yourself able to make your discernments without physical touch.

On practicing this with animal pets, you may be surprised to learn that you ARE INDEED able to swap feelings and thoughts with dogs and cats, although you may find that dogs are more readily communicative, and readily responsive to mental pictures.

III. Let us refer next to the experience reported of Paramhansa Yogananda in his book "Autobiography of a Yogi." There it tells how he would go out, sit quietly for hours at a sitting in front of a statue and focus his attention on it until he contacted the Spirit of that Statue, the thought form or inner aliveness which was behind it or built into it by its builder. *You* CAN DO THE SAME THING, given his dedication and time and interest to follow through. However much or little you do, you will find that you will sooner or later be able to perceive down into the soul depths of those glorious products of the Hands of God, meaning of course your fellow human beings.

As you find yourself increasingly able to sense the inner thoughts and feelings of other persons, you will find that you do NOT NEED to go to bed with them to have as fine a rapport as is possible for humans to have. If a compulsion to bed another person is evident, suspect deep trouble of a different order lurking in the heart or subconscious mind, which should be ferreted out and released, for the good of all parties concerned.

Now we do not say it is going to be EASY TO DO all that, but
IT IS AVAILABLE . . . and it works! If you desire to enjoy all that
wonderful—appearing human 'cake' . . . 'cheesecake' . . . around you,
learn to savor same MENTALLY, SPIRITUALLY.

"On becoming able to tune in on the wavelength of your cake . . . your
object of delight . . . you will find that you NO LONGER NEED to
ravish it physically . . . to eat it. It can remain there for EVERYONE
to savor.

"This will be found to work on baked goods as well!

"Now, between you and me, it is a wise idea to learn to sublimate
your feelings of instant rapport, however strong, however glamorous,
from whatever origin. Do not *suppress* your feelings, but confront
them, enjoying them inwardly, without physically doing whatever may
come naturally. The human is not taught to look behind the facade
worn by most persons. Behind that attractive creature may lurk the
Devil's Grandmother! Were you able to perceive just a little behind
the veil, you could see FOR YOURSELF, without indulging in
exploratory means via sexual misadventure to find that the veneer of
beauty hides Hell itself! Were you able to see all that, you would have
little difficulty at all in knowing whether to cherish your marriage
vows, and otherwise pursue your pre-incarnate goals for this lifetime.

"We now seek to introduce a simple but very powerful tool for
protecting yourself against unwarranted or unwanted intrusions, as
from other persons whose value systems may be inimical to yours.
We offer you the power to sidestep and/or counter invasions from
whatever source. At this point we do not seek to establish what YOUR
moral code shall be, at least to the extent that we are not going to tell
you that you CANNOT or MUST NOT indulge in the preliminaries
of sexual flirtation. To be happy, a person need not learn how to make
love in the most professional ways, although opportunities are openly
available. We would opt for tenderness! We SHALL, however, inform
the reader as to the relative merits of extramarital participation, outside
of matrimony, as there are indeed certain permanent spiritual values
which would be retained, if understood.

"Let us start off by insisting that it would be well indeed for young persons to receive sexuality instruction, and perhaps a certain degree of coaching BY RESPONSIBLE PEOPLE WHO KNOW WHAT THEY ARE DOING. In the European Aristocracies of bygone eras, a premium was placed on the sexual education as well as on the scholastic and the social education received by the swains and the debutantes, so that subsequent court marriages were most likely to be successful in the political scene. However well it may have worked out overall, there were certain pitfalls then, pitfalls which confront persons who are tempted to enter such an arrangement. Matrimony by itself, then, by no means guarantees confining one's wiles to the privacy of one's own marital chamber. Indeed, often the teachers and their adept pupils became and become enamored of each other, with continued liaisons long after school is out.

"As things turn out for planet Earth, the contacts established between bedroom buddies seldom are severed at death, continuing into following lifetimes. In other words, karmic ties are formed, bonding souls together over the eons. In fact, some persons have been chasing each other around the planet Earth for millennia. It is not necessarily all bad by any means to have one's earlier playmates accompany her or him in future incarnations. Most humans set up succeeding lifetimes together anyway, through family or adversary relationships of various sorts. But sooner or later it becomes important for the growing soul to begin cleaning up his aura, unchaining himself from the webs of sexual intrigue so that spiritual on-goingness can be cultivated in the larger or spiritual sense, on higher levels.

"Then let the idea of being able to have your cake and eat it be modified, updated a bit, to read 'You can have your cake *without* eating it!'

"The exercises we have provided here in this book are aimed at helping you regain and retain control over your emotions, your feelings, and to balance out your lower appetites with something that will more than compensate for appropriate expression of the Gift of Life. Included can be your mastery of the Gift of Sexuality. In other words, you can master Sex instead of becoming its Slave.

"Tantra Yoga properly understood and properly cultivated, offers homo sapiens a tremendous gift by providing a formal manner of approaching one's ideal Love Nature, overcoming lust by spiritualizing it, by transforming it into what seems to be superhuman or Christed Love.

"Now, for undertaking a proper program of development of one's total self so that human life and sexuality can be more greatly enjoyed, let yourself expect to become aware that you are becoming *more aware* of LIFE ITSELF, and that your enjoyment is thus NOT AT ALL LIMITED by or to gonadal expression.

"Alas, too many persons stop when they gain just a modicum of improvement in their sex lives, then missing the greater joys that lie beyond. Once you become able to perceive the subjective FEELINGS OF LOVE flowing between two persons, physical sexuality as such segues gently. It becomes nice but unessential. You then can go around and greet SUITABLY all those former flames, those present-era gorgeous hunks of female or male flesh, knowing that you could share in sex if you wanted it, but that to engage in sex would not provide anything any better than you already have at home. You thus can save yourself a lot of the time and resources when seeking sexual expression surreptitiously the old way, the Adam and Eve way, the missionary way, the HARD way!

"To experience all there is, PERFECT YOURSELF to RECEIVE it. As you come to realize the illusory nature of human relationships, your *whole* life, not just your *sex* life, will become transformed . . . more or less out of this world!

"We have given you criteria by which you will be able to recognize and respond to a former playmate. You undoubtedly made choices at the outset of this incarnation as to he or she with whom you will wed and work out your life problems. Stepping outside those agreements is fraught with difficulty for all concerned. Somebody ALWAYS GETS HURT, and seldom to a constructive end!

"If jealousy and a marital rift do not ensue, karmic ties alone will probably require a replay and recasting on the Stage of Life in a later incarnation. On the other hand, for "doing it right *this* time," you may never have to come back to Earth at all, having found something vastly better. Or, you can come back and name your own conditions! You can write your own ticket!

"Then seek to perfect your love life with ONE partner. When you can love one intensely and successfully, you could love them all. But by never really getting to know any ONE person well, you will never be able to love ANY person to PERFECTION!"

CHAPTER

7

Toward A More Perfect Union

"By seeking the highest fulfillment you have ever heard of you align yourself to receive it . . . and you may have to work through a lot of illusion to find it. Once found, it may be found elusive to keep.

"Humanity places a high premium in seeking and finding a perfect coupling, thinking to find it through ideal sex. Because there is more to it than sex however well experienced, even after marriage that search often continues. Down deep within, the human spirit is seeking its ultimate and mystical reunion with God. The pressure for continuing the search is always felt, looking for that elusive and intangible 'something better.' Until Man recognizes what it is that he seeks, he will continue scattering his precious resources of Time and Energy exploring byways and techniques, meditations and potions, and trying clandestine relationships with various persons of the opposite sex. In fact, that search is the story of Man's search to return to The Father's House (God). It has occupied Man's existence since shortly after his Fall from Eden, at which time he lost that oneness, that transcendental sense of Unity.

"In his search for reunion with The Father in Heaven, Man is slowly finding how much more there is to living the life of a Master than trying to keep up with Us and Our admonitions. By trying to read, understand and heed our words, the persistent seeker will find many things to be doing than struggling merely to keep body and soul together, important as that is. If it were not so, we would not waste our time or yours, and would tell you so.

"As things are going today, it has become vitally important that we be found telling Humanity about the myriad unseen and unknown things that most persons neither recognize nor understand . . . things required for his or her own evolutionary furtherance and deliverance from the wreckage he leaves in his own wake. We shall need to make much more noise as regards preparing Humanity for living that necessarily fulfilled life. To the extent we succeed, to that same degree our readership and clientele will no longer consider Death as an enemy, and many will no longer experience it!

"Our more enlightened readers and clients surely regard said overcoming as a goal more important than rubbing two bodies together in sexual expression, more than a specious or secondary goal for the present incarnation, as it seems generally to have been regarded.

"We then do not mind being found a bit repetitive. Our present approach is one of dividing up and yet expanding upon the general Game of Life into two necessary halves, separated but integrated. We do not mind the appearance of requiring that you should actually set about to live two separate lives . . . one portion spent in eking a life in the flesh, while also abstractly searching for the heavens. We too found ourselves living the life to satisfy Caesar, but we superimposed on it the necessity to emulate the Christed Life. Unless each candidate for serving as a conscious co-worker through the veil will seriously take up the yoke of that double life, even though surpassingly good human relationships have been experienced, much of long-term consequence will have been forfeited in that incarnation.

"The aspirant-candidate for finding the Perfect Union through Sex is in a difficult position. Being unable to make forward progress through having an improper set of goals, by default Man almost surely positions himself for falling into the trap of endless reincarnation. To help our most attractive candidates avoid that circumstance actually REQUIRES that we shall undertake the most strongly worded sales campaign of which we are capable. Do you now understand why we write as we do?

"Most Earthlings will not stir unless threatened by loss of a treasured thing, person or opportunity, or from fear of what might happen if he does not do a certain thing. Often the threat of an unknown punishment is more compelling than a known punishment for failing assigned chores. Sometimes we find it useful as a goad that we appear to threaten our student-aspirants with what will surely happen or will not happen if we find them lax in one or more critical areas, as WE define those areas.

"But seldom do we succeed for long in awing anyone into making of himself that paragon which is required for a person to be successful in working transveil. Unless we are truly successful in presenting our side of how things look from On High, we are unlikely to succeed in attracting and holding anyone to sacrificing much of what makes the flesh life seem attractive in the first place. Unless we can make it *more* attractive to be found working LIKE THIS, through the literal veil which separates Man from his Goodness, we are not doing at all the job which we agreed to undertake for YOU OR The Master.

"Our most demanding chore is to make the through-the-veil experience seem so real, so genuinely close to the objectives of any truly serious candidate, that it will be found compelling for one to pick up the threads of the Trek Heavenward. One has but to be adequately convinced that he has both the opportunity and the talent for becoming such a paragon. Almost every step of the way, we then need continue with selling each qualifiable applicant on the idea of himself being christable, yea verily, perhaps most of all, on the verge of being so anointed.

"To achieve that objective working from these subtle realms requires careful exposition of our case, as it is not easy for most persons to persevere in such a demanding undertaking, when being led from ephemeral sources. Therefore, we take our recruiting campaign seriously. While we may appear to be and are in a selling mode, we are also ideally qualified to represent The Heavens in all its necessary glory, and yet to sell our readership on the vital necessity to commence living as if its own goal in life was exclusively that of attaining one's own self-christing.

"Only when a person becomes convinced of the ultimate value in revising his methods and approaches to living does it become possible for us to commence reminding that soul meaningfully, that presently living-in-flesh spiritual being, of his literal value and ultimate responsibility to himself. And only upon being successful in helping that incarnate soul-being to change himself from the inside out, as well as from the outside in, shall it be possible for us to reward him or her with seeing and experiencing the formerly hidden special aspects of life.

"Human spiritual evolution and unfoldment are usually slow to manifest. Awareness of the subtle realms usually comes about so gradually that we cannot suggest that any particular talent or capability shall be rewarded for only having given up this or that former urge and its expression in flesh. Not until a person *no longer desires* to exercise the old former debilitative or addictive habits and practices can he or she really be considered as being safe to expose to the Inner worlds. We risk compromise and double-duty unless we undertake to ascertain who is developing the requisite inner strengths, and who is actually willing to undergo the strenuous preparation, while offering through suggestion, what the usual route to self-perfection entails, without discouraging them entirely from making the effort.

"It is an individual thing, this preparation of one's self for experiencing all that Life has to offer . . . this living the so-called Life of Christ, as it is more or less truly defined and labeled. We then do not mind telling you who read this lecture, that if you decide to go all the way Home, you will likely make a few changes in your present method of living . . . perhaps changes you had never considered. And yet, doing so will not appear at all as devastating as might at first be considered. Thinking on their effect, one is in a good position to make those changes voluntarily. We are cautious not to oversell. If anything, we are perhaps likely to undersell, to understate our case, and for good reason. Seemingly as a fitting record for having used the 'soft-sell' approach, we are most likely to have successful candidates, a higher success ratio among those who yield to our beckoning.

"We are not minded to fret too much if our general messages are read with mild empathy or outright antagonism toward our goals. Many persons who will be likely to read our epistles do so without understanding, or lack the ability to follow through. To Live the Life fully requires a greater sacrifice of the little ego-self than most people can sustain. Acceptance of those sacrifices will usually result in subtle improvements in life-styles, but are not usually accepted without a necessarily high degree of conviction or sincerity. We surely recognize that there are a few among your ranks who are more or less willing to experiment.

"In later life, or when a person has put away most of his former toys, those things which previously had held him to the Wheel of Rebirth, we usually have little difficulty in assisting said persons to hew to the mark, encouraging them to take up traveling the narrow pathway which leads to eventual Freedom. To call it Freedom surely paints the desired image of a person having become able to roam the skies untrammeled by the former restrictions of the flesh.

"Surely, the offer of power to roam the heavens at will, and to peer into the mysteries of the Akasha will seem great enough, glamorous enough, to attract many persons to sign up for the course on the spot. However easy it is to attract many persons to undertaking the necessary program of self-preparation, it is yet another thing to transform that willing candidate into a successful initiate. We cannot make anyone an initiate merely on his agreement without first aiding that person to prepare himself properly to become opened into the heavens. We should surely be suspect for even suggesting that we would do so without preparation. It requires that a candidate shall EVOLVE THE READINESS for such adventures, doing THAT by overcoming self. Without having overcome certain of his or her human foibles, it is not permitted for us to awaken a soul into the through-the-veil experience, out of consideration for the safety of the human soul.

"Each candidate for living and functioning in the Heaven Worlds must qualify himself for that role, for that capability. Nothing we do shall directly force or convey that ability, nor can we forge his papers as being qualified when he or she is not. We then are indeed GUIDES, helping escort seekers reach and pass through 'the pearly gates,' at a time when he or she has become readied through demonstration that he is able to assume personal responsibility by PREPARING *HIMSELF* for said entry.

"We often cannot find it within ourselves to promise becoming an overnight clairvoyant to the casual onlooker who will take up with our program of self-development. We can and do promise to help an interested candidate to recognize what presently is holding himself or herself back from such capability. Even when we have successfully told said candidate or interested onlooker exactly what he or she has yet to overcome or to develop in himself, it is still unlikely that such powers of travel or observation shall become at all soon evident. It is unlikely in the extreme that such development could be realized quickly without paying an unacceptable penalty, which is neither merited or worth the price of a sacrificed incarnation.

"As given now and iterated so many times throughout our discourses, it is possible but not safe for a person to work alone to open himself to the Tantra current flows and enter into the Heaven Realms quickly, without adequate preparation. The penalty is usually mental derangement, and is sometimes even worse than that, in that possession is almost a certainty. Without doubt, that would make life such a living hell that we go to almost any necessary extreme to assure that our potential student avoids the dangers in trying to force his awakening.

"There is yet another reason why we do not urge our students to take upon themselves any more activity than they could handle under almost ideal conditions. As you are surely aware, almost ideal conditions are seldom found anywhere on the planet Earth. One must then literally make of his or her environment that testing ground in which it becomes possible, however slowly, to develop those strengths of spirit which will permit *gradual* transformation of self above the temptations and ailments of the flesh side of Life. Once a person masters his own reactions and responses, he becomes capable of surmounting almost any human difficulty. Opportunities abound for a person who has overcome self to apply the benefits gained from working with us in The Heavens to take on some comparable level of expression on the material planes. Once having experienced Life in the Heaven Realms, Earth activities can no longer support the same degree of interest they did when one's only option was life in the fleshpots.

"Once a person has literally seen the Light, it becomes possible for us to enter into his consciousness that additional encouragement which is often found adequate for helping such persons to go the last mile in developing their own christed selves. But unless we find those persons and help them to know where they are in the Eternal Scheme, it is unlikely that they would succeed in finding and following The Path by themselves, or that they would recognize where they are and make the few but required changes in their present approach to life.

"We then are still recruiting! But we are still trying to be both candid and enticing enough to suggest to those already near enough, not to get hung up on Tantra, but to do a little more work and rise directly beyond Tantra into Heaven Consciousness. We offer an approach which will guarantee the fullest literal success. We find, again and again, that the only safe method of approach for a nearly-qualified Earth-person is to tell them both sides of the story. We show them as well as we are able, what their potential is, while still encouraging them to experience their remaining Earthlife lessons still needing to be resolved.

"Entry into either or both of the Tantra and higher degrees of so-called heaven consciousness is then not at all an easy thing for most persons. Those elevated levels of consciousness are not so readily found as a capability among one's friends and neighbors as to be considered a talent seriously to be sought. One then needs gradually to discover for himself, through study of tomes such as these, or/and through exposure to opportunities which shall be pointed out from time to time. One then gradually overcomes his limitations and then gradually experiences new degrees of freedom. As a person qualifies to enter into the higher levels of spiritual experience, almost imperceptibly he becomes aware of his increased capacity, and of the fact that her or his Service opportunities and duties have been increased.

"Whenever we are minded to (begin anew to) undertake rescue of one who has a lifelong pattern of asking in prayer for his or her release, perhaps already alternating between advancing and backsliding, we take special care to find ways to enter into that person's awareness opportunities that can be witnessed, experienced, and to look into special conditions, to undertake some side-venture into the realms of the relatively unknown. We say it again: for most persons to seek short cuts onto pathways not ordinarily accepted is usually to court disaster, and is at least apt to be costly in delays of unfoldment. Yet, unless somebody *does* undertake to inspect or to inquire into seldom-used or unfamiliar pathways like ours, he can hardly expect to make enough judgmental ability to discern or to apply consciously whatever experience he may already have accumulated.

"We are often minded just to offer each possible candidate enough good reading material and enough unsolicited invitations to attend meetings and special out-of-character lectures, so that to refuse becomes almost a cop-out. To refuse is then almost uncharacteristic of anyone working with us at these levels. We are not minded to overlook an occasional 'free shot' when entering into the consciousness of someone with whom we might truly become affiliated. But we also sometimes make use of other means of attracting attention to the very potentials of the human being through use of special psychic insights as another attention-focussing device.

"In other words, we do not overlook using anything legitimate which will attract a person's attention. What he or she does, once the attention is attracted, becomes entirely another story. But unless each potential candidate believer becomes active in the sense of committing himself to preparation for service at the highest sort he or she can accept, he cannot expect to develop those resulting finer essences which are truly required for one to become functional in the so-called hidden realms behind the veil.

"You may recall, even without considering yourself clairvoyant, having frequently witnessed persons who are unusually suave in their personal relationships. You may also have recognized persons possessing an almost distressing ability to sense what you are thinking, or who seem to know something before they have had the opportunity to learn it through conventional channels. You surely have met or heard of persons who possess an ability to heal the sick of mind or body. And you surely have experienced persons who are blessed with the talent for getting things done on a large scale, seeming to have unlimited energy and powers of persuasion, short of using brutality, of course, . . . persons who are the genuine leaders in the local or national sense.

"Few people indeed will take care to note what it is about said persons which entitles or enables possession and exercise of such talents. It may seem obvious, and rather quickly so, that anyone born of woman should equally possess similar qualities. It is truly stated, that what one person can do, another can learn to do or become. ALAS! If he or she only knew how to acquire those traits more easily! Yes?

"With this much of an introduction, we are suggesting that anyone who is willing to undertake just a little more work than the typical Earth person can discover many things about himself that makes him so human or inhuman. And he will surely quickly discover what he needs do to become as gifted as any other practitioner he has ever seen.

"Upon learning what said aspirant could do, he or she will surely undertake to discover what he has ALREADY BUILT that he could use or develop for Tantric expression, or could develop and perfect, which would make of his present lifetime a maximally rewarding experience.

"Once a person becomes interested enough to study the generic human being and its potentials for both good and not-so-good (evil), he will surely become aware of what it is that he needs do to let go of the nonconstructive stuff and cultivate and perhaps fulfill only the higher of his own capacities. He will also be learning how to let go of those traits or addictions which have been holding her or him captive to the flesh and to the earth-life. Given again, until each candidate aspirant strives to become the highest we can teach him, he truly IS obliged to continue returning to planetary life.

"Perhaps one of the best ways we can approach anyone at all interested in self-discovery, interested in undertaking development of his potentials for higher degrees of perception and performance, is just to continue in suggesting what is the normal experience for developed persons. For having become interested enough, we find that many persons will eventually make fundamental revisions in their methods of approaching living. Such persons become broader mentally and socially, expanding themselves and their capacities for experiencing greater happiness from life. The usual route is to dedicate themselves by undertaking study, discussion, and practice of those factors which will usually enhance one's ability to live harmoniously with his fellow Earthlings. For doing that much, or even that little, he becomes more valuable both to himself and to the world. And for once having become more valuable in the larger sense, he becomes increasingly of value Up Here as a Co-Worker with us. We then can set his foot in a higher rung on the ladder, on The Pathway with us to Ultimate Perfection.

"Do you take adequately to note our use of the term 'Perfection?' It is quite literally the situation that self-perfection is the only pathway that leads successfully to living the Heaven-Life, whether lived on Earth or in that supposedly out-of-body or 'heaven' life that is thought usually to be available only after death. We are here to suggest to you that lack of or bypassing the traditional physical death need not at all prevent a person from experiencing the so-called 'heaven life.' In fact, we are trying to suggest that only those persons who have become perfected enough, who have successfully overcome ego-self, are able to experience everything of the Inner Life, from whence the so-called heaven-life is derived and lived.

"It has always been difficult for us to find new ways with which to convince any of our readership of our thesis, whether in the present Earth-era, or in any of those past eras in which we were privileged to live and work and to participate with you. The same old problems arise in trying to awaken the slumbering flesh-man anywhere in Time, as we presently find things. You then should expect us to approach the situation with use of all the means or methods which were found successful anywhere at all along the Time Dimension.

"We have demonstrated to our satisfaction that the former sheltered ashramic approaches to learning of and functioning in the upper worlds are but seldom appropriate for the contemporary Caucasian and Aquarian-Age Earthling. We are no longer able to depend on an aspirant picking up the cudgel of self-discipline, just because his Master said to do so.

Today's aspirant needs to have some very good reason for doing so. We also have found that it is nearly impossible for a person to become interested in studying the metaphysical realms without it having some longer-term influence on his or her thinking. We then do not hesitate to suggest that anyone who is really interested in finding how far along The Path he or she has traveled, can (and probably will) undertake all the research possible to learn of how such things (as constitute the Tantric inner realms) can exist, and of how such things are and have been experienced and transcended, literally from the commencement of Time, in that way finding himself.

"Anyone who wishes to learn more of how a person can experience health, happiness, wealth, or a special talent, or perhaps the opposites of these, shall do no better than to read and to study the experience of those many great souls who have traveled this way before him.

"What one human can do, another can duplicate. However, for that to be experienced, an aspirant to a duplication of said feats or traits of character in a neighbor or a competitor, should take into account very carefully whether there be any merit in undertaking such emulation. It is then incumbent upon any such aspirant to examine very carefully, reviewing what he or she is trying to do, when perhaps there are vastly more important goals to attain than getting hooked on Tantric Sex. Now, Tantric Sex is not at all a bad place to be hung up, but going on directly the rest of the way up requires perhaps least expenditure of Time and Effort, if one is dedicated to achieving relative perfection or self-christing.

"By exploring wider horizons, one may perhaps then find himself possessing some valuable talent which had previously been latent but suppressed, or which had escaped note. For all this to be discovered requires only that each person, aspirant, or candidate for living life more victoriously shall first undertake Study of Self, and follow through wherever it leads.

"We end this morning on the note that nothing in the world can be, is, or ever could be of greater ultimate importance to an aspirant than undertaking the adventure of LEARNING WHO HE IS, of his divine origin, and of how he or she may consummate that trek to Perfection. As Perfection is approached, gradually one learns to function in increasingly higher realms, finding that he never has been outside that state except it had been in his own lack of SELF consciousness, in his lack of cosmic consciousness.

"Enough?

"We rest."

8

Levels Of Human Sexuality

"We recognize five levels of Love, of which Masters may experience four. Some people experience three levels, and many experience two. Of course, everyone on Earth considers that he or she is expert in all matters pertaining to sexuality, from recluse to courtesan. From having lived oftener in the flesh and having had differing experiences, some persons do indeed have more aptitude than others. Some of it may have been refreshed, perhaps because of childhood exploitation or indulgence, or for having had greater opportunity than most. And of course there is a noted variety of opinion, depending on the manner in which one has gained said wisdom—experience, whether vicariously as through Old Wives' Tales or neighborhood gossip, at the Locker Club, from a book or TV video tapes, the man or woman next door—whatever. Direct experience is of course ultimately the best teacher of said All-Seasons favorite indoor sport.

"But because of implications well beyond the basic reproductive act itself, Sexuality is a topic not to be considered lightly. It is well known, if not widely accepted, as the one force in the universe that everyone else is made familiar with, preceded in importance only by two other human forces. These of course include Survival, and the dichotomies of Feasting and Famine, plus Pain and Pleasure. Everything else is considered as secondary, to be explored or not as interest and opportunity present themselves.

"This morning we intend offering fresh insight into one aspect of that greatest of all forces labeled LOVE. Now . . . Love contains several widely acclaimed subsets of Sexuality, along with certain important but usually unrecognized manners and matters effecting its expression. Then just settle back and take our discourse as it develops, taking it at face value, as worthy of experimentation as the urge strikes you.

"Three identifiable levels of sexual expression are the Physical, the Emotional, and the abstract level of human Mind-Spirit. Where it is possible, we shall differentiate between them, because it may not be obvious to many persons that each level of expression blends from one into another. Ideally all three levels are recognized and enjoyed. Human reproduction on the physical level requires male ejaculation, so that the human race shall continue having flesh bodies available for its ongoingness. After that purpose has been served, we identify second-level interplay for profit or pleasure, or to satisfy deep psychological or emotional needs for expression and relatedness. It is perhaps less apparent the extent that sexual expression takes place in the realm of fantasy, more so 'between the ears' and less 'between the legs,' although there is some intercommunication between all three levels.

"Consider how often that both physical feelings and emotions become heavily involved without orgasmic response. Many females report pleasure in sexual intercourse through involvement of the more abstract levels of participation. When indulged in circumstances of respect and affinity, these include the feeling of being adored, sharing in and giving love to a loved one, being needed, found attractive, including the stimulative closeness of body sensations. Please note that here are examples of human sexuality transcending the physical and emotional levels and rising up into those higher realms, approaching and entering the spiritual domain. The higher levels offer an infinite reservoir of joy and well-beingness, available for drawing and capable of being experienced by those persons who have learned to reach into those heights. Their qualities may be identified, approximated by calling them names like Rapport, Unity, Concord, Affinity and Perfect

Love. Then where one degree of expression begins and another leaves off is not always clearly cut, nor is it likely definable without serious study, nor is it always necessary!

"Of such we sing, as we discuss further introduce how said higher states may be experienced more perfectly and frequently.

"It becomes important for a person to be familiar with and experience the unusual but higher levels of Sexuality, if only because there is so little written about it in the literature. Anyone can find almost anything in print about the subject of Sexual Intercourse, from Sunday School lessons to Tantra Yoga, from any aspect he or she can imagine, but the element of Love is considered to be an intangible. Many persons are willing to teach other persons *about* Love for a fee, vicariously, or by direct rehabilitative physical exercises. Thus one quickly 'learns the ropes' in handling himself and herself mechanistically in the everyday world of physical human sensuality. Whether the learning experiences are pleasurable, emotionless, disgusting or frightening depends upon many factors, depending greatly on the purposes and circumstances in which the activity is undertaken. The range of so-called human sexuality then includes everything from Rape to Rapture.

"As we too have heard, one definition of the difference between Rape and Rapture is SALESMANSHIP, and in this we concur. The PURPOSE behind close human contact is in itself one of the most important elements from which to view and judge quality in the transaction of expressing human affinity. Sexual expression occurs in all ranges from bestiality and habit, into affinity and the little-recognized aspects of spiritualized Human Love. Love takes place in different manners with varying degrees of success and satisfaction only as It is examined and understood and the findings invoked. Whether a couple participates grudgingly or willingly, or even joyously, with respect and appreciation and the afterglow of Love for having participated in a sacrament, or whether done for recreation, or from sheer urgency, procreation is still the intended outcome. Surely, the Grand Designers of the Universe knew what They were doing when They designed human sexuality!

"Let us now consider aspects of sexual love with which we are perhaps more familiar than most readers, due to our more abstract experience with it, having also had it all when we too were incarnate, and now seeing it from this side of the veil. We have a significant advantage over most of our readers in that we can tune in on sexual expression at all levels and in all its aspects, and observe our Earthlings in their joys and sorrows.

"If you wish to investigate further the several levels of repressed sexuality, let yourself consult the Bibliography, while we undertake here to offer some new or extended points of view. We are first going to offer some keen observations that are intended to help convince most readers that it is not at all necessary to involve one's sexual organs in expressing True Love. While use of one's sexually-related or aroused surfaces is usually involved to one degree or another, it is by NO means necessary to work to express Love in the higher planes through their stimulation or application. In fact, it is not uncommon for elderly or otherwise incapacitated persons to have not made physical love for many years, if ever, and yet retain a kind of affinity and appreciation which transcend sexual expression of the classical sort.

"One may scan the literature on Love and discover for himself that some of the world's greatest love stories and songs were written by invalids, by souls who or which could not respond by more than the sense of touch, the sound of a loved voice, or even more abstractly, by capturing thoughts of love in poetry or musical composition.

"As another means of recognizing the value in subjective levels of expressed affinity recalled, consider the value in a bouquet of flowers, in a simple note, in a memento. Consider, if you will, the cleanliness of being able to express care and feelings by look or touch, by a mailed letter or photo or greeting card, or by telephone. Consider the volumes which can be spoken in a look or in a warm embrace, and the possible implications for persons who are already in a state of mutual admiration. Yet, these methods of expression, even though already well above the physical or emotional levels, pale in significance when compared to the Inner Fires of Life, that higher Sacred Fire which is observed to have such immense value and power in persons who are able to respond to Love on the higher levels, as with persons/souls who find themselves working Up Here in The Invisible Realms with us!

"If you are still following us, please consider that genuine Love reflects a high state of acceptance, accepting another human soul AS IS. One senses an undefined warmth and perfection, perhaps even while noting but accepting changes that would seem to enhance a deeper relationship. When no need is felt to make changes in the other person or soul or spirit, looking for and finding it, then a State of Love is at hand. A state of UNCONDITIONAL ACCEPTANCE of one soul by another is probably as high an interpretation or definition of Human Love as we can provide in written form like this.

"In the higher planes there are energy flows, finer essences, in the human aura and mental fields, flowing in and out of the human structure, connecting one person to another. These take place but are discerned consciously by only a few people. When those same fields and currents are felt issuing from a person but are not recognized for what they are, that person can be said to be sexy, or charismatic, to have 'presence,' or to personify Love. When a person learns of the Finer Dimensions of Feeling, and then learns consciously to experience the Love Force, he or she sooner or later recognizes that he is now dealing with *spiritual* Love.

"It is possible to refine oneself, to hone one's sensory systems, to the point where it is found that Perfect Love can readily be shared, indeed rising above, sublimating, and transcending need for sexual organs and orgasms. *Indeed, sexual involvement on the flesh levels can spoil an otherwise ideal relationship or spiritual reunion.*

"Indeed, powerful affinities can and often do carry across the Gulf of Reincarnation. Appropriate expression of strong personal attractions carried over from former-life loves requires proper recognition of present-life relationships, lest prearranged present-life opportunity and precious All-Time affinities be damaged or lost.

"There are times when feelings of oneness can be experienced, shared, or enhanced through a lingering embrace, a hug, by clasped hands, a handshake, or even an implied caress from gentle use of touch. But there are also many times when it is neither possible nor necessary even to embrace or touch another person. Sometimes Silence is Golden, times when a spoken word could spoil an otherwise magical moment. Much indeed can be communicated through deep eye contact.

"They who wish to experience the subtler satisfactions are able to develop and realize the higher degrees of expressed affinity through conscious practice of subliminal communication, and as well by attempting conscious communion through gentle but minimal use of touch, caress, soft words, practicing eye contact, and telepathically, through thought and feelings communicated WITHOUT DIRECT or IMPLIED USE of the human sexual apparatus at all!

"In the hearts and minds of unregenerate spiritual beings, of humans who persist in returning to the planet Earth, perhaps the least happy are those persons whose sense of self-esteem and self-acceptance are dependent solely upon their capacity for bullying, and their ability to express love or affinity through use of their sexual equipment. These will be found to include application of the urge to control others via the social and the sexual machinery, whether used between male and female, between male and male, or female and female. The difficulty, the long-range trouble, is then found to stem from the deemed necessity to demand physical means for expressing what is essentially an instinctive or spiritual connection. It then should not be at all surprising that one meets dissatisfaction when it no longer is possible to maintain a macho image, or for one to use those time-honored forms of relationship for expressing feelings of attachment or demanding same.

"There are also other levels, other processes which impose barriers on satisfactory expression of love or affinity in its many degrees. Such barriers lie in one's psychological makeup, usually buried there below conscious recognition, sometimes serving as protective barriers against experiencing pain, or to hide from one's own past. In other words, it is becoming widely recognized that personal inadequacy feelings which bar proper and satisfactory expression of friendship are hindered from being sought and found by the difficulty one has, classically, in facing anything at all that is painful . . . much more so on the psychological levels than on the physical pain levels, where pain can oft-times be reduced or eliminated through medication.

"For many people, effective medication for an aching soul is very difficult to obtain, or put into practice, because of the general lack of mental control over one's accepted considerations and conditions of body and mind. It is found that one deficient in control over his own mind finds himself in the clutches of robotic recorded habit patterns lodged in his subconscious mind. While we have surely beaten this topic to death elsewhere, it is found to be so prevalent a condition among incarnate humanity that the concept can hardly be told too often. Humanity MUST become AWARE of its blind dependence upon IMAGES, on RECORDED SUBLIMINALLY-OPERATING HABIT PATTERNS. These are the stimulus-response patterns whose nature it is to evaluate the constant barrage of our human sensory perceptions, and to initiate automatically the built-in reaction processes to the many stimuli we experience unawarely in our everyday occurrences and relationships. There is little spontaneity possible when it comes to expressing feelings and thoughts with and to another incarnate being, especially when one DESIRES to express LOVE *for, to,* and *with* that other person.

"The LEVELS on which Love can be expressed, and the forms such expression can take, are dependent on the levels of attention one can focus on and maintain CONSCIOUSLY. For most of the world populace, these tend to be limited to the lower levels of mental development, to those whose development has been stymied or otherwise limited to the lower levels socially experienced, or gained in flesh life. We are telling you that only among persons whose mental and intuitional development have been raised is one seemingly capable of having such clear-mindedness as to be able to RESPOND to the finer essences of Thought, at the level of the incarnate Human Spirit, wherein the finer keener perceptions of Love can be realized.

"Ideally, in a young marriage, a proper balance of good physical condition, coupled with purified emotional responses, topped off with intuitive discernment is required. Such persons so able and engaged or involved are able to approach that perfect balance which assures the greatest overall impact of Love Expressed, Received, Acknowledged, and Returned, which does most for the human race.

"For developing the capacity to sense the energy flows between the male and the female chakras, one is able to discern exactly what is needed to assure the greatest, the most fulfilling interchanges of

Divine Love. Tantra Yoga, properly mastered and used, enhances one's ability for having each related and respective chakra opened and the energies flowing, interchanging the inner-soul feelings and communications that truly unite True Lovers in Spirit. One thus qualifies to experience that perfect oneness beyond Tantra, told of by the masters of all-time, and sought by most souls/persons who interrelate through sexual intercourse, finding that highest of all knowable pleasures. Their degrees of mutual response are then dependent on, and are an accurate indicator of how well one can find Love in its higher senses.

"We are able to witness those current flows, so have little difficulty in assessing wherein a person's overall makeup causes difficulty. We are correspondingly able to help a Student of Life discover and overcome barriers to his fullest Life Expression. This should be reason enough for one to search most deeply how he or she can experience Life, living Life More Abundantly, to quote the Master of Nazareth [John 10:10].

"A person who is willing to undertake and to experience the processes found necessary and effective can release the human spirit from its bondage to the collected human ego and its recorded programs which control his expression of incarnate/physical life. He and she thus *can* find Love AVAILABLE to them on the higher levels, and more richly than are conventionally experienced. Then, when finding that your life expression is changing, consider yourself to be growing in your ability to express life in SPIRIT, not then being limited or subject to control by a composite of lesser or egoic levels of programming.

"Expressing True Love involves POLARITY on HIGHER PLANES, quite a different experience than is available on the usual physical or lower astral planes.

"We are providing you with ways to judge FOR YOURSELF the relative ability and importance Sexual Expression has and should have in YOUR life as a way of experiencing BALANCED SPIRITUAL POLARITY, and how you can go about finding and satisfying it at the highest possible levels.

"Aye!"

CHAPTER

9

Relative Values

"Most people in the U.S.A. have to get out and sweat to make ends meet. Yet, there is far more to life than just money-grubbing for an existence. Even so, the daily grind presents Man a marvelous opportunity to *learn how to live*. You can learn Spirituality while you go through the motions of making your living, whether it be laying bricks, repairing something, doing your bookkeeping, teaching school, whatever . . . by proper attention to your relationships, while working at whatever is your form of service. The important thing, then, is less how much time or money you have in your life, but what you *do* with what you *have*. If you use your opportunities only for accumulating money, you'll probably be well enough off to provide comfortably for your needs and still have something left over for worldly pleasures or other pursuits. But if you live only to make money, during your post-mortem self-examination, you may find that you've wasted much of your life, having failed to take advantage of your opportunities for *spiritual growth*.

"From the spiritual standpoint, the traditional goals of mankind are rather sterile. Earthlings are necessarily intent first upon providing their families and selves with the necessities of life, such as food, a roof and shoes. But many go on to seek luxuries, such as a pair of shoes for each day of the month, gourmet dining three times a day, several private mansions, foreign cars, prestigious jobs and titles, and community standing. Others set their sights on accumulation of massive wealth. Yet the achievement of goals beyond the bare necessities seldom brings the sense of fulfillment expected.

"In the end there is always the feeling that something is lacking. When people become dissatisfied with Life or with themselves, they tend to blame their unrest on somebody or something else, . . . on having married the wrong spouse, on their sex lives, on their business associates. Yet, all the while they continue seeking elusive Pleasure from exploiting materiality or their body. And still they are not happy.

"Although Man's traditional goals for himself are not necessarily bad, they should be the result of careful consideration on where they fit in a larger setting. Early in Life, Man should seek to understand what *are* those objectives that will bring the happiness and the spiritual growth he supposedly came to Earth to make.

"One of the most effective ways to research this question is to proffer the answers in a familiar religious frame of reference, tying them into the Bible and showing that these problems and their solutions have been known for a long time. The following typical Bible quotations are keys to successful living, good for all times and circumstances. If you learn their meaning and apply them in your approach to life, the end result will be rewarding.

—"Fear not, little flock, for it is our Father's good pleasure to give you the Kingdom" [Luke 12:32].

"At first glance, this seems to bring up even more questions, since it doesn't sound like Heaven is something you should have to strive or struggle for. Why, then, are you working so hard, if Heaven is *given* you? Why do you not experience it now?

—"You have not (received) because you ask not." [James 4:2], and

—"Whatever you ask of God, He will give to you" [John 11:22].

"If you have asked and still have not received, perhaps you have not asked properly, from James 4:3, 'Ye have not because ye ask amiss.'

"From these collected admonitions it should be clear that you must learn WHAT to ask for, and HOW to ask for it. Here again, your forefathers have anticipated you: 'If any man lack wisdom, let him ask it of God' [James 1:5]. Gaining WISDOM, then, seems to be the key. If people took advantage of their opportunities to seek and obtain Wisdom, or even Knowledge, they would *find* fulfillment [Matthew 6:33].

"A person also can ask for Light, the Light of Understanding; without that Light you could spend your whole life spinning your wheels, looking for the wrong things, creating your own sources and forms of unhappiness. Each human has enough inner light to guide him in his next step. But part of that step should include asking for *more* light, and the ability to *recognize* what you will be shown. That is the beginning of Wisdom. As written by Solomon, 'Happy is the man that finds Wisdom, and the man that gets understanding' [Proverbs 3:13]. And further, 'Wisdom is the principal thing. Therefore, get Wisdom, and with all thy getting, get Understanding' [Proverbs 4:7]. And to think that all these things were recorded thousands of years before Christianity and Psychology came along!

"It follows from all this that the direction in which lies the ultimate happiness, associated with the idea of Heaven manifested right here and now [Matthew 4:17, 10:7, and elsewhere] can be found in the search for understanding of *self*. For understanding yourself and how you interrelate with your world, you will come to understand *right thought* and *right action*. Right understanding, then, leads to all the other 'right' facets of life, including right diet, right exercise, right work, right play, right attitudes, and right relationships. We can say that all these things constitute fulfillment of the biblical word 'righteous.' If you investigate that word further, you will find that it stems from the quality of 'rightness,' or being free from error: hence, it is directly associated with Wisdom.

"Never fear to bear the tag of 'righteous,' for it is the highest possible compliment. It does not connote, as so many people seem to think, that you are some kind of 'goody-goody.' Contemporary society tends to look down its jaundiced collective nose at anything having to do with getting the most-needed qualities in Man's approach to life, those qualities of Love, Compassion, and Joy which provide happiness and success. To the contrary, those very qualities, put into practice, will lead to the highest attainment in the sense of achieving what we call Heaven Consciousness in the here and now, with well-being as a by-product.

"Then it seems to be a case of 'First things first!' After all, what could be more attractive than the promise of attaining that state without sidetracking yourself from the pursuit of the normal but dubious and fleeting happiness and pleasures of the world ?

"One of Man's most difficult tasks and important goals in life is to learn how to see things as they really are. When you go about getting material things and qualities, it is of the utmost importance that you be able to recognize especially the *relative values*. Most of you are fully aware of the *idea* of relative values, since you use this concept in your daily decisions, in selecting your daily necessities and relationships, in pursuit of material things, position, or power. In that process, there are values, decisions, and pursuits that are *con*structive, and there are those that are *de*structive. And there are decisions that are relatively good or relatively bad, although people do not always pause to consider which is which. And even when they make 'wise' decisions, they often fail to implement them.

"So much for the goals. To take advantage of the implications of this message, you will need to get started. To help you start, this series of discourses shows one how to understand the wealth of published materials that are available for study. Such materials take many forms, but are made readily available to the layman through 'Pop Psychology,' a popularized study of the human self and soul. Excellent paperback books and pamphlets deal profusely with the subject of self-understanding, on how to relate to one's compatriots, and how to improve all facets of life. Community evening adult schools, some churches, and many special groups increasingly are providing more and more courses in self-understanding.

"Let us talk ACTION for a while.

"The key to successful study of the relative values in Life is *learning how to look at your SELF*. Since your problems begin in and remain within yourself, it follows that you should begin with a STUDY of your SELF. You must learn how to examine your thoughts so that you can recognize what thoughts you dwell on. You must learn the difference between true *thinking*, a process of searching and correlating your mind/recordings for something specific . . . this as contrasted to just letting your mind free-associate.

"Another major key to success is the ability to observe your *feelings*, and to learn how much they are influenced by what sort of thoughts you *allow* your mind to focus and dwell upon. A natural part of this process is then to recognize whether you are causing your own feelings, or allowing them to be caused by someone or something else. You will gain great insight into how you face your own world when you recognize how your thoughts and actions affect the thoughts and feelings of your compatriots. You will learn that you are really dictating almost everything that happens to you through your own responses to your situations and opportunities.

"You may be surprised to realize that your world is totally responsive to YOUR OWN convictions. Furthermore, you will someday recognize what your convictions really are. Even as Job said in Chapter 3, verse 25, you will find that whatever you dwell upon (in Heart and Mind and Soul) will become your experience. When you become aware enough to realize that fact, you will be well on your way to mastering yourself and your total life circumstances. In the biblical sense, you will have overcome the world.

"This will literally be true, since *your* inner world is different from everyone else's inner world [Job 3:25]. Perhaps it is fortunate that there are no two identical persons!

"It is important to recognize that your circumstances are, for the most part, of your own making, either through direct action and confrontation or through default acceptance of your environment and attitudes as they are. We REPEAT: you, individually, must ultimately recognize *how you continually create your own circumstances*.

"As we have said before, according to the Bible, every human was made in the image and likeness of God. This would seem to testify that we all have some degree of God Power, with the relative ability to create things in your OWN image and likeness. Thus, if you do not like your conditions, perhaps you should find out how you are creating them . . . your own circumstances . . . and strive to change them. This puts the burden right where it belongs . . . squarely on you.

"But enough on the subject of CAUSE AND EFFECT . . . on making choices by understanding RELATIVE VALUES. The remainder of our discourses will be devoted to examining how to go about *understanding* how you create, viewing yourself as PRIME CAUSE, seeing how you interrelate to other similar members of the human race, i.e., and how you therefore apply your own God-given powers.

"If you have occasion to read other of our publications, you will note that among our many discourses and admonitions we present specific methods on how you can follow through with freeing yourself from the prisons created by your attitudes, allowing yourself to be transformed by the renewal of your MIND. Through the tremendous power of focussed attention, applied in the area of developing and directing the subtle course of 'The Energies of Life,' we will show you an approach to Ultimate Fulfillment by integration of two diametrically opposed philosophies. When viewed from On High, Tantric Yoga and Asceticism (whether of Christian or Mid-Eastern) will each be seen to have achieved similar, if not identically the same end results . . . spirit freed from attachment to the Universe of Mass, Space, and Time.

"As you shall note, we have integrated those two approaches into a composite method which we believe will be recognized as the shortest route to obtaining and experiencing the Joy of Perfect Freedom which is so great an element of Heaven-ness.

"When we have finished our discourses, you will discover that we have provided you with means by which you can pose questions directly to us and receive appropriate answers. You will have Light in making proper choices among relative values, even as you go.

"You have but to bear with us. OK ?"

10

Let There Be Love

"The strokes are getting shorter!

"By allowing one's innermost thoughts to free associate in the area of Relationships, it becomes possible for an interested person to find what it is about Love that It shall be allowed entry into Life, let alone that It should be explored. And then conversely as well, for the havoc that Love can generate, it becomes feasible to undertake examination of what it is about Love that it should be allowed to play any part in Life.

"It has been said that the pen is mightier than the sword. That observation will be found to be true when both are tried in the attempt to win the fealty or love of another person. Then, as long observed in the writings of the famed warriors, orators and penmen of the ages, it is often their love pieces that have survived, and that so often continue to hold a high place in the surviving literature.

"The works of Elizabeth Barrett Browning a century ago bear out our observation, especially as found in her expressive poem 'How Do I Love Thee? Let Me Count The Ways!' It shall not serve us well at this time or be necessary to enter into an analysis of her longstanding works, but many survive in collections which also grace the minds and hearts of the souls whose minds are able to roam freely in the Heavens of Thought and Feeling.

"Similarly, it is found that the Music of Love survives the incrustations of the ages, surviving as well the ravages of political and economic systems. With the advent of commercial recordings and their worldwide distribution, electrical playback facilities with the miracle of radio and the electronic theater, more-so than ever before, Love is presented in forms whereby it becomes possible for an entire courtship to be conducted through Illusion, through the private fantasies of each party to the relationship.

"The 1930's and 1940's saw the era of the Great Bands and Light Opera, the many Andre Kostelanetz and Jeanette MacDonald-Nelson Eddy renditions of Love during the pre-WWII, and compositions like 'Falling in Love with Love.' These typify what has always been possible for would-be lovers, to romanticists who cling to some inner dream of a special life with another dream person. With today's Rock Music, marriage, when it results at all, often stems from little more substantial than that. Logic as an element in the selection and mating process tends to be limited to the middle classes and the wealthy or intellectual classes. Increasingly often, it is Illusion plus Emotion that dictate one's state of sexual expression.

"We then note here that it has long been possible for anyone whose mind is clear, a person who is found capable of contemplating the finer essences of the Universe of Life, to use the Spoken Word eloquently to convey feeling almost as easily as it is to use it for bringing Light or for creating any particular effect in the Universe of relationships. Even if not thoroughly cognized, such persons might experiment with his and her creative potentials by decreeing 'LET THERE BE LOVE,' even as God is credited with having created the Universe by saying 'LET THERE BE LIGHT!' A person then may stand back to observe the subtle processes as they enter his or her environment, which by the way, is essentially how the fundamental aspect of Life in this Galactic Life System originated.

"The First Cause and most powerful identified force operative in this Life System is Love, energized by the Spoken Word. So often, creations from the spoken word follow the ramblings or semi-coherent feelings or patterns of the subconscious heart, modified by the contemplations or musings of the semiconscious mind. And often even these are given precedence over a thought held silently. Even though thought forms are powerful, focussed thought is necessarily less powerful and takes longer to reproduce itself in form than is the spoken word. Alas, the magic of silence is often broken by speech, aye! But as the prism catches the fundamental white ray of sunlight and breaks or expands it into a myriad of colors of various shades and hues, of tints and bands of coloration, so it is found when the integral Force of Love is examined, that each of the fundamental three color components, as defined for convenience, is related to subjective or mental conditions. Each color of the spectrum serves well to capture and convey energy, as is done by words, but the actual subjective *feelings* of a human ego or personality incompletely voice a totalness or integrated view or purpose.

"Let us examine the three primary spectral colors of red, green, and blue, to see how the fundamental Force of Life is applicable when examined in components to assess the human condition.

"RED is used to express power, anger, or strong lust, as conveying a strong state of energy used more to express aggression than to express subtle feelings of a subjective nature, characteristics attributed to softer shades and pastels.

"A person 'feeling BLUE' is conventionally considered to be out-of-sorts, to be sad or moody. Yet, the same coloration is also considered as serenity and to be a fine and fundamental healing color by some practitioners. We might find that certain tints are more effective than fundamental Cobalt Blue, but that matter can be perused in the literature.

"Let the basic GREEN be examined casually for the implications inherent in its nature. Green is usually associated with Life verdant, representing abundance and freshness. Green fields and forests are usually associated with burgeoning life, and is a much welcomed coloration over the browns associated with the passage of life, as from Spring and Summer into Winter.

"When integrated, optically and electromagnetically speaking, the combination of the three basic or primary colors adds up to White, the color of Completion, of Spirit, or Purity, the fundamental creative energy of this Universe. Mixing pigments produces quite opposite colorations!

"Whenever we are minded to examine other in-between shades in the continuous spectrum of white light, we marvel at the smoothly changing coloration or wavelength aspect of that fundamental force, whether called Light or Love. Love issues from certain higher spiritual octaves above the observable processes of Physics. Like love, it is learned that there is no one particular dividing line by which one level is separated from another, and therefore that Light and Love then synonymously are found to contain a broad range of uses, for harmonious and special applications.

"It is well known that various colors of light generated by heating metals do indeed produce different effects in the life systems of plants and persons than when that particular color is produced by chemical pigmentation. Growth becomes more rapid in the presence of certain bands or wavelengths of radiant electromagnetic energy than by reflection and absorption from pigmented coloration, and can be hindered by their lack, or from energy concentrations in foreign color bands.

"In a metallurgical physics laboratory, coherent light observed by spectroscopic examination demonstrates that certain colors are always produced by certain combinations of elements. However, a metal ingot being white-hot in a metallurgical sense means that its energy temperature (around 2500 C) is at the blue or high energy end of the light spectrum, higher than the energy temperature at the cooler or lower-end red colors. In fact, Physical Energy flow manifests by running from high energy invisible ultraviolet sources down through to the infrared. A heated ingot tells us a lot about itself by its physical energy-coloration, noted to have colors of light blue, pink, yellows to orange, and on down as it loses energy by radiation down to frequencies invisible to the human eye. Energy-wise, there is a correspondence with the spiritual colors, themselves measured by special effects associated with special colors.

"In the realms of Physical Chemistry, certain interactions exhibit a stable affinity. Particular colors produce catalogued psychological effects when standard pigmentations are used in making paints from certain standard chemical compounds of certain elements. For example, Chromium and its compounds produce shades of yellow. Compounds of copper can produce greens and blues. Compounds of cobalt produce blue, while compounds of iron produce reds, and so on down a lengthy list. Pigmentation-producing quasi-metallic colorations sometimes have uses compatible with the effect also produced psychologically by their electromagnetic light counterparts, depending on the emotional or psychological effect being sought, or produced in the aura by one's emotional state. Pigmentations then produce or influence a certain range of emotional effects, which may or may not conform equivalently to the effects produced by their invisible spiritual counterparts.

"In fact, when radiant energy received from distant visible stars is examined under powerful analytical spectrometers, it is found to exhibit light and dark bands at certain points on the color spectrum. In this manner, the colors of stellar emissions are used to determine and to analyze the composition of the star itself. Then what appears to the eye as white light is apt to differ significantly, one star from another, as regards what said celestial body is made from.

"Correspondingly, the presence of those same metals or technical elements can be identified, depending upon how much energy was used to bring them to a radiant state. The composition of that same unknown substance or piece of metal becomes discernible by observing the radiant energy produced when the element is heated to a temperature high enough to emit light. When the heat is on, we all show our true colors!

"A trained clairvoyant can make similar uses of the various colors found in the human aura to determine the nature of a person's talents and ailments, but too few such resource persons are available.

"On the lowest levels of Love, even a human is said to be 'in heat' when sexually aroused. Said condition of arousal in itself *is* accompanied by a higher energy state during normal social conditions.

"Astrology, whether considered as an art or a science, also assigns various characteristics to the Love relationship, associating the quality of Love to the individual planets, even to including their associated colors and metals, along with their psychological and physiological aspects. Their consistent correlation and the wide acceptance of those qualities is an attribute to the overall integrated nature of Life, whether expressed as Love, or as some other quality.

"The interested social, physical, or spiritual scientist is thus enabled to use the fundamental colors of the spectrum to analyze the various forces present or absent, active or inactive, by observing the place they occupy in the light spectrum.

"We then can summarize that the colors of the differentiated fundamental energy of Life convey and contain almost magical properties, depending on how the initial energy is generated and applied. We then can prepare to investigate a few of the stronger colored energies which we shall later in studying Tantric and Spiritual energy flows.

" 'When you are hot, you are HOT!' That phrase is often heard at the gaming tables, in the stock market, on the football field, etc. It is also applicable to one's relative ability to heal, as when bringing colored light, light of the appropriate wavelengths, to bear upon a specific situation or ailment. Here also, higher energy levels correlate to the healer's ability to bring massive ailing areas or ailments to higher temperatures and lighter colors rather then due to coloration alone. Being 'hot' then equates to the ability to bring greater quantities of Life energy to bear than can the lesser or lower energy states.

"A few old timers have seen pieces of iron being heated in a blacksmith's forge. When cold, they are black unless polished up, of course. When heated they become familiar shades of red, orange, yellow, blue, or white depending on the amount of energy brought to bear. Rather than assigning the qualities of that piece of iron based only on its color, there is a more basic assessment, because one seldom applies a piece of red-hot iron to heal a physical condition needing *red* energy! We then observe that the human energy condition corresponds quite accurately to the relative state of *emotional* heat or *mental* condition or harmony present, indicated both by its etheric color quality, and by the quantity or intensity of the radiation which is present.

"When a person is heavily intellectually oriented, he or she tends to like the shades of yellow, perhaps with tints of red. Indeed, the aura of a genius mathematician is observed to contain larger quantities of yellow around the head than usually witnessed around humans. A physician is apt to radiate light green colors predominating in and around the auric head. Color truly is a very useful aid to the trained clairvoyant diagnostician to discern the relative development of the human mind, or in its absence, equally well indicating a lesser degree or lack of mental development.

"Hence we observe that the predominant color(s) in and around the human aura readily reveal the basic orientation of any person being examined, as well as their physical, emotional, and spiritual status.

"Note that the pure color red represents a high energy state, but its direction of expression varies greatly in different social, emotional or psychological settings. When a muddied brown and a deep or scarlet red is found in the lower sexual areas, it of course represents potentially a highly charged state of anger or sexual excitement as lust.

"An aura containing blacks, grays and/or browns is indicative of unhealthiness in some aspect of the person's life, including particularly the relationships and the ability to Love. The color red seen throughout the human aura is likely to show livid rage, the victim perhaps literally 'seeing red.' Little surprise then is attached to the toreador's use of red flags to excite his prey, or to the use of red flags and lights or banners to indicate danger or blood. From these brief examples we correctly observe that colorations carry with them excellent diagnoses of the state of mind in the human aura, attesting to one's true spiritual nature or condition. His or her preferences for those same or similar colors in matters of dress as a rule frequently convey deeper psychological states of beingness, permitting one to use color charts for approximating one's psychological state-of-mind or mental condition. Indeed color charts are used for diagnosis by some therapists and counselors.

"In matters of the heart, in Pure Love, one then should expect to find subtler shades of color, of pastels, to represent the finer forces and shades of meaning and sensitivity. The hues in between the Red and the Blue ends of the spectrum can be found to contain an area rich in violets and turquoise, of mauve and azure. In these ranges of the spectrum are to be found resident the gentle and delicate tints and hints of balanced inner feelings. Indeed, with the services or talents of a well trained clairvoyant, one who can associate the observed and discerned feelings with the colors themselves, one may swiftly and accurately diagnose a loved one's form of discomfort. At that level of perception it is also discerned that the color fields do not remain stationary, but reflect the evanescence and ever-changing thought forms and colors of the active human mind. Dull minds tend to show weak colors, to be grayish cast, and sluggish in movement. It is then easy to diagnose a person's personality at a glance.

"When a lover or a poet tries to define his or her physical surroundings using subjective symbols and colors, perhaps to probe the Essence of Life for symbols of Love, said symbols often are found to reflect the colorations of the morning and evening skies. Flowers and trees and other classic symbols of a promising new life are imagined to be facing all lovers, and are projected to represent the promise of unfolded committed love manifest. The skill and imagination with which one lover can use symbols to share love fantasies with his or her loved one then indicates their mutual responsiveness to the subtle degrees and relative sensitivity to matters of lower vibrations. If equally perceived, their responses would be useful as well to indicate their respective future depths of mood swings and aspiration, of Hope.

"When a person is minded to do so, he or she can find the colors of Love almost anywhere and everywhere. It is in the developed capability for discernment as a way to focus attention 'where the other guy is coming from' that marks the differences between Heaven or Hell experienced. Any two persons who are on or above the same or similar wavelengths can respond easily to the state of mind or heart possessed by others similarly inclined.

"Such available portents of Love lived in the flesh unfortunately are seldom considered or noted by the lovers themselves! Lovers have a language all their own, operating on special wavelengths and systems of reference which serve either to unite them or to separate them.

"One's preference for colors indicate accurately the character he possesses. Although one's selection of coloration for clothing is somewhat dependent on the nature of a social situation, office practice and protocol or economic status, or political circumstances, there is still that fundamental preference for colors which complement the aura, the soul of the individual. Such preferences recognized then are themselves useful to show a person his relative appetites and preferences for Love or Sex in its various temperature ranges, too, while also useful in healing!

"There are spiritual temperatures as even there are social climates and temperatures. One fundamental difference will be the strength of the colors, like red, as compared to the finer etheric colors of pink, or at the other end of the scale is found the indigo of the saddened personality or spirit. What passes for Serenity in the realms of the spirit is then apt to be misconstrued as 'feeling blue' or non-responsive in the lower human realms.

"Then one's responsiveness to the various states or wavelengths of light are indeed capable of being indicators of one's literal State of Being. Other states are then capable of being stimulated by appropriate uses and mixes or color. That fact is well known, and is exploited routinely applied by some Healers, by the advertising media, and by decorators and painters of buildings, and on the artist's canvas. The poet also tries to capture Love by painting word pictures, hoping to capture alive the subtler feeling levels. Indeed, one's susceptibility to the use of word pictures is a direct measure of his or her spiritual inclination, receptiveness, and ability to respond.

"The ability and capacity of one human being to stir sentiments in another human through use of oil or watercolor paintings or music compares favorably with the susceptibility of each soul to respond to wordpictures. In either case, one must be well along in his or her mental-spiritual development to find himself responsive to what has managed to be handed down through the centuries as either great painting, art, drama, music, or as great literature.

"We are attempting here to make a clear distinction of the levels on and at which LOVE as a subjective experience is capable of being expressed. We hope to have shown that there are DISTINCT LEVELS, wavelengths, for the expression of Love, and that they range from a basic urge for sexual release, all the way up and through what a human can catch and replicate in paintings and or with words, on beyond into the nonverbal levels. Then, one's use of language and song as an expression of Love is an excellent indicator of one's spiritual state of evolution. It thusly should be so considered by one who would seek to understand Love in its various guises, and to express or fully convey abstract or purely subjective feelings fully with his or her object de amour.

"Love is then truly seen to be a many splendored thing. Love is available and can be expressed on all levels, although in some cases we would hesitate to dignify the many varied expressions we see used by associating them with Love.

"Perhaps least of all understood, and certainly least advertised is the difference between PERSONAL love, as compared and contrasted to TRANSPERSONAL love. To the left of center on a logarithmic (exponential) scale we shall define Love as a way to express degrees of personal caringness through shared use of human sexual intercourse. This form requires physical bodies to send and to receive said feelings. And who indeed is to deny purpose and effective communications on that level?

"But when the human ego becomes involved in expressing affinities on the physical level, there is apt to be found the feeling of ownership, and the experience of hurt feelings. Yet, to the right of center on the scale of human Love is the idea of a burgeoning Universal Love . . . a love which does not require human flesh for expression. Indeed, further to the right of center (to the right of the Origin), involvement of human flesh can deaden the response as too gross. Yet, the higher levels are available mostly to they who have *perfected themselves* for *Love* in *Spirit*. In between are all the levels which Humanity can conceive.

"Very talented persons have written and sung songs to express love. Some persons can express Love beautifully through exalting the sense of touch. Both are exalted when combined in the classical song 'How I Long For The Touch Of Your Hand,' composed and widely aired in the mid-1930's. When a physical separation hinders direct expression, even the sound of a loved one's voice becomes a powerful means of conveying feelings, whether by telephone, radio, television, or recordings, and even an old photograph or a love letter or keepsake is something to 'tune in on.'

"And who has not experienced thoughts of a distant loved person, whose imagination or fantasies set up and maintain powerfully attractive Force Fields through mental exchange of the Energies of Affinity with that other person. An as yet unexplored and seldom mentioned means to express Love is through the conscious use of Thought Forms of Love, deliberately generated and sent from one soul to another. So powerful and pervasive is the Energy of Thought that feelings are conveyed readily in and among one's circles of friends and business associates.

"Truly, loved ones are never alone in Spirit!

"The range and depths of feelings expressible in that little-considered manner of telepathically communicating affinity is largely unexplored. As a field for research, it is nearly inexhaustible, and the energies involved are quite capable of sustaining Life itself. Indeed, it can be stated both accurately and clearly that the power in one's mental state of affinity is in direct proportion to the degree that he can generate and respond to *spiritual* Love. Here indeed is the very basis of psychic healing, of giving absent treatments . . . from being on similar or coherent wavelengths.

"As said earlier, the wavelengths and power of human feeling are observable to a trained clairvoyant in the colors, balance, and strengths of one's chakra activity, and in the overall size of the general auric ovoid, but the levels and the purity on which a person is seen to be operating, on which a person can respond to or generate Love, are thus likely to differ greatly from one person to the next.

"However beautiful the sentiment, the difficulty in rising above Personal Love to reach and embrace another person in Christ-like or Transpersonal Love is perhaps greater than would be accepted by those who teach of the quality of Love at the highest levels.

"When attempting to discern whether another person loves YOU, perhaps by determining their ability to respond to the love YOU send, or hold for them, it is important first to inquire into several more of the larger broader interpretations of what Love *is*.

"Examples of the more intellectually or spiritually oriented affinity are available through study and pervasion of the poetry of Elizabeth Barrett Browning, and of course the works of many others. Perusal of such classics basically shows Love to be a composite of feelings and activities which stimulate elation, and hence is largely an intuitive or an illusionary function of the creative realization process. Perhaps one of the best ways to gain immediate enlightenment is to open a Thesaurus and see the many shades, modes, forms and definitions Love can take.

"Love surely includes caring for the well-beingness of another soul or person, whether close, known or unknown. When a parent takes the trouble it is to raise a family, it is a sure indicator of Love Manifest. But when a person can feel equally responsible for the well-beingness of an entire planet full of humans, THAT's AMORE! Obviously it is not feasible to make physical or sexual love to a world full of humans, so there must indeed be a broader definition than the vulgar expression that 'love is between the legs.' or 'all in the mind.' Obviously there is more to it than that!

"Indeed! Love on the higher levels is capable of being experienced and practiced in marriage, even when Love is not expressed through sexual intercourse, but through fundamental caring . . . through the little things . . . perhaps like between a brother and sister, or parent and child. It is not at all necessary that sexual intercourse be used to express devotion, affinity, or that innuendo of same be communicated to express the desire to Be One with another person or personality. But few people know the difference!

"Infatuation, sometimes called puppy love, and honored in song as 'Falling in Love with Love' is a familiar state of affairs. Not at all limited to teenagers, a person is sometimes enamored with the feelings generated in his or her own psyche. Usually he or she is blinded, unable to perceive the exact or true state of affairs within his psyche, or to observe that there is only a one-way situation existing between he and the object of his amore. Such an existing state of affinity will seem to demand that some sort of expression be communicated and reciprocated between them.

"Discovery that both parties are unequally aware of the imbalance in their respective feelings, or are not equally able to express, receive, or return affinity causes much disillusion. An unequal ability to experience or express Love is then frequently a major cause of distancing between married couples, or between persons who might otherwise marry, or affiliate in some other manner, perhaps sexually, or musically, or even just jogging together along some mountain trail. "For the general well-being of persons habitually in close proximity, a proper understanding of what affinity or Love is should include the consideration that it is fundamentally a caring, less so an emotion, and only secondarily or remotely involving sexual expression. Much of the difficulty in human relationships can be avoided when persons realize that it is indeed both POSSIBLE and NECESSARY for persons to widen their definition and acceptance of Love as both a natural phenomenon and a cultivated state of being. Whether sexual intercourse is used or shunned, or is set aside for practical or more esoteric reasons, is less important than that each party learn to RECOGNIZE and to ACCEPT and to PRACTICE giving and receiving comfortable expressions of care, and possibly higher feeling. It is then vital that persons of Earth be able to accept the idea, the phenomenon, that one person CAN love MANY others, and not just one and only one alone, as so romantically taught.

"Again, how many persons do YOU know can love THAT impersonally?

"Much of the marital stress widely observed today arises because each party (or perhaps only one!) was taught that he or she cannot LOVE or BE IN LOVE WITH ANYONE ELSE at the same time. The social pressure of that concept has been largely responsible for keeping many a family together, for keeping either mate from wandering elsewhere in the presence of shared affinities. However, it also has been responsible for a great inner distress and halfhearted support of one's mate and/or family unit, and yes, the root cause of marital rifts.

"It is time to take note that there is a great difference between Love that requires or expects restricted sexual expression, and Love which permits random reciprocation of expressed or communicated affinity. One's availability, in or out of wedlock, is easily expressible through facial expression, through gentle touch or gesture, and is often communicated through the eyes as an unvoiced knowingness. Truly, as in the silent screen movies, there is an abundance of ways to express a very large measure of one's personal feelings without words, through which great spiritual growth can be gained, transpersonal love exchanged, and care made known.

"Many humans become adept at reading silent signals, and are on the lookout constantly for signs that one's spouse is indeed communicating Love to another person of the opposite sex, thereby threatening the status of the suspicious party. And indeed, some persons have developed skills in using silent communication to express open availability, to test one's attractiveness by enticing an attractive person, to seduce another human of the opposite sex. Indeed, the entire social world of today seems designed to support glamour and to encourage the witchery of sexual attractiveness by stressing oppositeness. It seemingly ignores the more lasting mature values of Mind and Soul, of Spiritual Development, over the emotions and the so-called Heart.

"Until more persons become aware of the actualities and implications behind the fact that most human affiliations are based on impermanent emotions and physical attractiveness, there remains the possibility that a third party can be attractive. Infatuation, viewed as attractiveness, seems dependent upon superficialities, a third person possessing talents, capabilities perhaps less possessed by one's present mate, whether those seeming assets originate in a questionable 'Hollywood-like' social value system, or from not having recognized what is worthy versus what is impermanent, therefore not recognizing what should be shunned.

"More persons are attracted by glamour than from past-lives affinities. However, when affinities carried from past-lives are augmented by glamour, we often have an irresistible force apt to be the cause for broken present-life vows. When a person has incarnated to marry a particular person and crosses with a former lover, sometimes it becomes very difficult to hew to the present-life social mores, to fulfill the obligations accepted in a planned present-life affiliation.

"Feelings of attraction and antagonism *are* carried across from one life to another. It is seldom appropriate that such parties resume their former alliance. Perhaps equally often, old sparring partners reunite, having scores to settle which originated many lives earlier, requiring marriage to draw them together again as the means to work them through.

"We then find that Human Love can be expressed simultaneously on at least three and often on four levels. The more able one is to express Love on each of the levels, the more successful are likely to be the marriages, living together in permanence, happiness, and making expansive growth in further and deeper expressions of loyalty, affinity, and love. This opens up the potential and necessity for learning how to express Transpersonal or Impersonal Love at the same time and with the same persons that one expresses Personal Love. In that manner, it should be seen possible to love ANYONE on all seven levels available to Humanity.

"When a human decides to attempt learning Impersonal Love, it requires diligence in examining his feelings and responses, his reaction to any particular object of attention or attraction. That is not necessarily an easy thing to do at all, since humanity has so long been taught the *lower* levels of affinity as being the *true* levels of expressed love, instead, being taught erroneously that Affinity and sexual love are identical.

"Now, to some degree, Love contains Affinity as a subset, but neither Affinity nor Love need require sexual intercourse for its expression. It may sometimes be difficult to perceive the ever-so-subtle difference between the desire to support and live with one's mate if married, to feel like attending a Significant Other person if not, and the more practical desire to be just special no-strings-attached friends.

"It is hardly found possible within the present makeup of most persons to be able to differentiate between the desire for sex with someone and the feeling of just wanting to be with them. Too often there is a great gulf between the two life expressions, so that the sexual manner of expression leads to deeper commitments of which neither party is able to or can readily accept. Then, the necessity to learn the difference between PERSONAL LOVE, INFATUATION (love of love itself) and IMPERSONAL LOVE becomes vitally important to all the parties concerned.

"Enter here the concept that the capacity to share the same Space and Time and Energy with another soul is as close as it is possible for the Human Spirit to experience Love. Then how to achieve that circumstance necessarily forms the remainder of our endeavor for this book.

LOVE AS PERFECT ONENESS

"Now that Mankind is entered into the Aquarian Age, it is vitally important that persons on the pathway of spiritual development learn early-on that LOVE as ONENESS is the key quality to be developed during these next two thousand years. Persons already sensitive to the gentle qualities but not yet to the Forces of Love are at a disadvantage, while yet having a peculiar advantage relative to persons who are unaware of either aspect to the dimensions of Love.

"A person who is already aware of his or her feeling of Love for another person to the point that subtle past-life affinities rise into the Present has the task of learning to accommodate and to transcend those feelings. Otherwise they risk damage to their present-life opportunity for a harmonious relationship. The classical human nature brings with it certain karmic responsibilities and opportunities for handling forces appropriately to one's present incarnation.

"While it is true that past life rapport is ever present to be dealt with, the lack of remembrance of specific detail of past incarnations brings with it a certain blessed insulation from the pressures to resurrect the original affinity. When properly exercised, so strong is the mating urge that it is often difficult indeed to separate out the cause of said attraction, while living out the responsibilities accepted for the present incarnation.

"Perhaps the most difficult of all is the ability to confront and to accept the pressures that uncompleted past-lives bring into play, such as pressures to escape present-life affiliation. Much energy often goes into avoiding the present-life relationship, regardless of the actualities of said previous affiliation(s). Since humans come back to Earthlife for the purpose of experiencing the conditions most favorable for gaining and expressing one's highest good, it is incumbent on all parties to recognize and cooperate with the complex and subtle forces which arranged their present marital pairing.

"When two marital partners are noncooperative it is sometimes found that their marriage relationship becomes Hell, even when akashic research discloses that previous lives together may appear more or less idyllic.

"That same couple, perhaps having met again in less desirable times and under greater difficulties, finds in their present lives the culmination of many unfilled needs and desires. For parties from each of two *other* marriages to succumb to the temptation to switch partners for what seemed idyllic in a previous lifetime is to work AGAINST an acceptable togetherness in the present-era lifetime. To change partners in midstream is probably to incur negative points in planning future lifetimes.

"Attempted use of sexuality to allure a mate from an already existing marital relationship is then asking for trouble of serious proportions, especially when it interferes with fulfilling the pre-incarnation planning processes. While humans have The Right of Decision, misuse of the Power of Love activated through the very potent sexual process does invoke the Force of Divine Creativity in keeping the human race alive and continuing.

"Then, the causes of the pressure for expressing an unusual affinity merits examination, especially when stability of one's marital affili-ation risks running afoul. ANY causes for discontent should be exam-ined and resolved. For doing one's homework in THIS incarnation, a re-affiliation in later incarnations may not be at all necessary, or attractive.

"It is necessary to have given the above discourse at this point because a solid background in the Power of Sexuality is required. The energies and power released through practice of Tantra and higher Spiritual awakening processes for social disruption cannot be over-stated. Nor can the relative unwillingness of the usual Human to self-discipline be overemphasized.

"Such is the Power of Sensuality."

CHAPTER

11

The Importance Of Sex

"Sexual intercourse can be a very creative act. It is capable of stimulating energies of a very high positive and fulfilling nature.

"On having entered the physical realms through incarnation on Earth, each human spirit becomes a personality to gain certain understandings, to accomplish certain deeds, to develop certain thought patterns, and to react and to participate in the three-dimensional physical world. While each such soul comes here to the planet Earth for different reasons, yet each ultimately seeks fulfillment via self-mastery in many different ways.

"Spiritual energy . . . Life Energy . . . has as yet to be defined and understood. When used only on its lower-scale dimension, as Sensuality, it becomes the feeble act of a Creative Being trying to find its ultimate Sense of Self by reproducing itself. In that way, human beings constantly thrust outward trying to find that perfect companion, to experience that perfect sense of fulfillment—that which would gratify the inner higher desire *and* the urges of the body.

"On a temporary basis, some satisfaction can be had with almost any other human sexual partner, but *only* temporarily. For you see, it is a grounding and a fusion that happens when said union involves only the lowest of the spiritual centers (the root chakra). There is

always that constant urge and desire to seek that greater fulfillment . . . the ultimate. As yet, very few souls have moved off the
lower levels.

"The polarity of Sex is vitally important to you human beings for
procreating and continuing your race. There is a whole realm of energy
ever available to you. And as a being develops and evolves toward a
greater sense of fulfillment, gaining a greater sense of unity and
oneness with the universe itself, it will normally consciously choose
to use that constant influx of energy for fulfillment on more exalted
levels. Such human being will choose to deal with it from the higher
centers, to plunge itself inward into greater depths of perception and
response and participation with life. And so, that being will not limit
the vital life force from flowing through a sex chakra, but will
ultimately reroute that energy and allow it to develop and work through
the higher levels of Mind.

"So then, is sexual intercourse a positive experience for the whole-
ness of the body, or is it a negative experience? It is both. It fulfills
those souls (who are) here to become bonded with mates, to generate
families, to learn of their own curious desires, urges, and passions.
Ultimately, as a soul evolves by frequent return to the Earthplane, it
will become more consciously aware of that vital life force. It will be
more selective in how it uses that Elan. Proper use of the Life Force
will move an individual beyond a limited Earth-bound sense of identity
and fulfillment, transcending a selfish perspective, to using that life
force for the well-being and the welfare of a good many more people.
It will consciously choose to activate those energies and to workout
of the higher chakras. [This is the direct objective of some Mystery
Schools.]

"Ultimately, everything becomes fulfilled, and everyone finds his
place upon the Wheel of Life. (In the Earth life-system) you must
move through a series of progressive life experiences. In other words,
the young soul will rarely come into the earth realm and immediately
successfully open the inner mind. It will come here to seek the basic
desires of a physical mechanism, and will seek companionship and
understanding on that level.

"Each time a soul-spirit reembodies itself, it will grow to a greater identity and become a more expansive functional part of the universe. And, each time that same fundamental unit of Life Energy will be used for a greater cause and a greater sense of development for many more people. Fulfillment is found in *how well* the opportunities and resources are used.

"The Sex function is vitally important to you peoples in that it is a natural part of the body, but it also is important to remember that you are here to learn to master its energy, and to master your own resources and use of Life Energy.

"And so, thus, as you become more 'involved and evolved' you will become more selective, using your life force when it supports and perpetuates your spiritual ideas, as opposed to using it at random or with carelessness through pleasure-seeking only. It can be used more properly as an expression of love, and of course it can be used for its designed function in reproduction of the human species. It is all in how you use it, how you nourish it. Ultimately the expression of Love becomes our finest expression. So it is both positive and negative, according to each individual entity in fulfilling his destiny, and why he came to Earth.

"We thank you for letting us come through."

CHAPTER
12

Views On Contemporary Sex Practice

"While this chapter may give some people ideas on sexual practices they have not tried, it was included to satisfy expressed curiosity regarding how contemporary sexual expression is viewed On High. It is offered for guidance of persons who feel great pressures for sexual activity, yet who are hindered in its expression by ancient shibboleths, social and biblical commandments, by physical problems, and lately by the fear of pregnancy and/or AIDS. Considerations of a more fundamental nature have also been discussed in our volume "So You Want To Be A Channel!"

"Spirit LOVES, while Personality LUSTS. True love needs neither marriage nor sexuality for its expression. The genuine article Love transcends either and both conditions, as when two people are united in spirit. Until that time, most humans will try their best, or worst, to find some aphrodisiac or substitute for the gnawing feelings of unrequited affinity. When enough people practice only the highest forms of sexual expression, there is hope for the rest of the world to find satisfaction. In the meantime, we offer points of view which may help reduce the confusion and help relieve some of one's felt needs for interim companionship through sensuality and sexuality.

"A wide variety of sexual expression is available, and is practiced with one or more sex partners, for longer or shorter periods of time, depending on opportunity, their health and state of mind. Disillusionment is the usual experience, plus accumulation of debts of a social, health, economic, and/or karmic nature. When improperly engaged, increasingly stronger measures appear required to achieve satisfaction.

"For a couple to achieve true satisfaction in the sexual phase of incarnate human life requires deep personal respect, total acceptance, and commitment, whether or not accompanied by mutual and simultaneous achievement of orgasm. Means for reaching that state are inadequately documented, and discussion of the possibilities here would leave much to be desired. Let word-of-mouth and other books suffice for the present.

"When pristine sexual intercourse is accepted and performed as a sacred rite of procreation, it is possible for the greatest interchange of metaphysical or spiritual currents between male and female, allowing sexuality to reach fulfillment on its highest levels. As a consequence it is apt to be a state infrequently realized, nevertheless one widely sought.

"Whether the participants in sexual activity are married in the sight of Man matters little when two are determined to couple sexually. That factor accounts for many couples incarnating to fulfill an implied agreement made in some earlier lifetime, when conditions may have been less favorable than can be had in their present incarnation. Strong affinities from earlier thrill-packed couplings account for a greater degree of marital infidelity today than might be believed. When a person is experiencing forces pushing for a sexual liaison, holding your feelings and your attention in present time . . . being RIGHT HERE RIGHT NOW . . . is the antidote to averting consummation of an otherwise imprudent venture!

"It is often found that when two persons experience strong temptation for sexual expression, they may have mutually well developed subjective or psychic sensitivities. They are apt to find themselves tempted more frequently and more strongly than are persons who rely on food or booze or chemically-induced lust for their sexual stimulation.

"We are stating, as clearly as we can through this communication medium, that sexual intercourse is more frequently used as a means to express frustration, boredom, or anger than it is to express Love or a deep affinity, and even less often than under any agreement to produce a baby body for a companion soul to return into present-era incarnate life. When sexual intercourse is used to vent the lower emotions, you can depend on incoming souls to be faced with lives of most difficult circumstances, who are more or less desperate to make up for past crimes and errors or to 'get even with' their former antagonists. Said category of participants then produce the least desirable sorts of incarnate souls.

"Note, however, that when copulating procreatively, accompanied by mutual feelings of affinity, the highest sort of soul is attracted. Especially will such be true when conditions for a returning soul into Earthlife are prearranged to assure the returnee opportunity to develop major specific details of personal, career and spiritual expression.

"If an absolute criterion were to be imposed on the success of expressed sexuality, it would favor preparation for the highest sort of new-life possible. Then whether sexual intercourse were entered by a particular husband-wife team, or with partners from another marriage, or without marriage, is less important than that a near-absolute parental affinity prevail throughout the appropriate life span of the participating souls, shared between those already incarnate and the soul desiring to reenter Life as a child in the physical planes.

"We then shall spend less time on contemporary or available techniques used for sexual expression than we shall spend on describing some of the processes which accompany and augment an ideal sexual expression.

"Ideal fulfillment originates in the invisible realms, when the life-currents flow unimpaired between one partner and the other, when each chakra is matched to that of his or her partner, assuring then the intercommunication or COMMUNION OF SOULS.

"The spiritual current flows between two spiritual aspirants are maximized when they are attuned, are on excellent terms personality-wise, whether they are married to each other or not. Said current flows can then be observed and shared by The Guides as spiritually harmonious, freeing them from experiencing anything but the afterglow of fulfilled affinity. THAT level and sort of activity is preferred on both sides of the veil. An aspirant to christing then need not be totally celibate, or confine his or her sexual performance to the marriage bed. Much depends on one's value system, and on one's ability to express affinity responsibly.

"A time will come when the use of the human orgasm to express affinity is passe. Whatever other forms of sexual activity Humanity uses to satisfy remnant desire for expressing affine love then matters less than that said couples shall continue working mutually to consummate their present lifetime together *on the highest levels*. This implies that their form of expression will expand into the legendary heights of Transpersonal or Impersonal Love, a level only speculated upon, and experienced by supposed masters of incarnate human life.

"If Spirit embodied in Human flesh can develop and manifest degrees of the ideal of being One with Life, and if said paragon were to share his or her presence with his associates, it is possible and becomes the norm for said personalities to become freed from any need to express sexually, as through use of the human genitalia. In effect, sexual expression is no longer required, having become a secondary manifestation of affinity, i.e., as a way to express impersonal love.

"We note that few persons now incarnate are able to transcend the NEED or DESIRE for sexual intercourse, whether expressing Affinity or Lust. When people who have been incarnate together in sexually active past-life relationships now find themselves bonded with others, it can be difficult to know how to confront and express the old feelings without renewing their former sexual relationship. A still-smoldering affinity can be identified and acknowledged, but is best satisfied by transpersonalization. It is then possible to enjoy those old feelings, once their origin and existence are recognized. There is NO NEED TO BE OFFENDED or obligated when a former partner appears again in your *present* life.

"Because former-life relationships were not always experienced or conducted in marriage, a person does well to recognize the CAUSE of unusual attractions, and apply proper ways to acknowledge the energies and to cope with them, as actors do when moving from one scene or play to the next on the Stage of Life. When engaged in a particular scene or act, in particular incarnation and marriage, give it all you have, knowing that your ability to express higher levels of affinity in future times grows in direct proportion to the care and energy expended in understanding how to express ALL THERE IS with one's PRESENT marital partner.

"All this is then to announce that we much prefer that the human sexual expression shall be consummated, yea, maintained through lifelong loyalty to one partner. We readily grant that one person can relate successfully, or seemingly so, with several lovers, husbands or wives . . . if not all at the same time, then sequentially. We STILL prefer that a couple shall indeed forsake all others, and strive to reach the highest there is WITH EACH OTHER. THEN and ONLY then is one most likely to transcend physical-plane lusts to SPIRITUAL PLANE LOVE.

"Let it be recognized that *Spiritual* Love does NOT require sexual intercourse for expression. However, if a physical connection and orgasmic activity seem required, there may be a remnant of LUST from chemical and/or social/personal stimulation. Only when LUST has become converted to LOVE can that couple be said to have gained all there is. With most persons now incarnate, that state of affairs is likely to be achieved a LONG LONG way into the future. The more intuitive any person becomes, the more spiritualized are their senses, and the more rapidly they can and should seek perfection of their relationship in all its aspects . . . good communication, total acceptance of each other as is, and being happy, willing and supportive companions along the way.

"Under such seemingly idealized conditions, it will be possible for a person to rise above the need to express sexually whatever level of affinity now is beckoning across the eons."

SEX PRACTICES

"We shall now discuss criteria useful in sorting out what practices should be and should NOT be engaged in the various sexuality and relationship processes.

"Lesbian expression of affinity, love, or just plain lusts for the strong feelings of the sexual orgasm, is more frequently encountered than perhaps even the lesbian community recognizes. By employing lesbian techniques, an impotent male can induce female orgasm without benefit of an erectile penis. For persons who are not yet aware of the differences in the male-female current flows involved, sexual gratification as a way of gaining fulfillment or for expressing mutual affinities, of one soul for another, may be found more readily achieved by female-to-female contact than by the usual inept male-female contact. This comes about because of the juxtaposition of the female clitoris, a small organ residing at the upper part of the female genitalia, the vulva. Unless special attention is given by the male to 'ride high,' contact with that small but vital organ is apt to be minimal, producing the common complaint among females of the "Slam Bam, Thank you Ma'am" approach attributed to male rabbits. Lacking that knowledge, some females become more satisfied with a lesbian partner than they are with males, augmented by classical female gentleness.

"We acknowledge use of masturbation by both sexes as a means for release and self-satisfaction, along with its pros and cons. Masturbation is commonly used when suitable companionship is not available, or physical conditions prevent otherwise normal release. Here again we call attention to the need to balance the astral/psychic current flows in the human aura, if greatest available satisfaction is to be achieved.

"When a formal working relationship has been established between an aspirant or chela (an accepted through-the-veil student) and his Guides, the latter keenly feel the sexual tensions and feel the methods used for release. Some Guides report displeasure from being forced to experience such low-frequency vibes, sometimes suggesting use of a surrogate means for closing the chela's sacred current flows. Because of the strong impact of their Chela's sexual activity on the Guides' feelings, celibacy is preferred. However, classical balanced male-female sexual intercourse is much preferred by The Guides over masturbation. Although a Guide is unlikely to be affiliated with a homosexual student, on the inner planes, female homosexuality is preferred to a male homosexual relationship. Both relationships have karmic implications. The Guides consider especially the male homosexual form of sexual expression to be an abomination.

"Stated again from another point of view, unbalanced forms of sexual activity do not provide an ideal closed system or permit a state of body-mind-spirit well-beingness, when considering the auric fields.

"When one has become accepted for through-the-veil training, it is well to note that his Guides and Teachers feel all the same feelings that the absent sex partner would feel. Guides sometimes complain that their spiritual connection, once established with a student, forces them to experience the lower lusts and sensualities which They had overcome, and which most personalities generate in their sexual activities. Then celibacy in the later stages of Self Development makes sense, and is encouraged if not outright requested, especially when an aspiring person is working alone.

"In summary, permit us to state that of the sorts of sexually specific orgasm-producing methods, we Guides prefer the classical as-intended male-female juxtaposition, with or without insertion of the erectile penis, with or without ejaculation, with or without orgasm.

"Of the nonstandard forms of sexual intercourse, the least objectionable popular form for ventilating affinity sexually or obtaining relief is the lesbian manner of expression. As a form for mutual masturbation, it is minimally capable of spreading disease or causing pregnancy, is gentle, and is then preferable to almost anything available to maledom.

"Last of all and least acceptable is the Male-male contact, Sodomy. As a method of substituting for traditional male-female intercourse, Sodomy has been practiced all throughout recorded Time. Of the methods available, anal intercourse is most likely to expose the participants to disease. Although permitting expressing lust and affinity, it is noted in passing that some males cannot accept affinity from or express sexually with females. The converse is also sometimes true in the lesbian relationship.

"A description of psychological and or spiritual methods for alleviation of addiction to such conditions is withheld for our last three chapters. However, the cure or release lies in the realm of seeking to know one's self, what a person does, and why he does it. Considering the long-term implications of reincarnation, ridding self of sexual hang-ups is a sufficient reason for undertaking counseling. But unless that counseling has an approach which permits investigation and release from past-life recordings and relationships, it is unlikely to prove significantly effective as a therapeutic release.

"Then let us finish up today with the observation that anyone who wishes to explore sexuality outside the sanction of his marriage usually does so at some risk, like losing whatever good start he or she may have had at the time of their betrothal. Whatever satisfaction a person or a couple may seem to find outside their marriage most often could indeed by found AT HOME, if the partners were dedicated to looking in depth into perfecting their mutual relationships as a joint lifelong project.

"Then to attain greatest sexual satisfaction, ideal sexual congress will transpire in safe, comfortable and secluded surroundings, when the participants are well fed and freed from fear, worry, haste, and fear of threats of disease and exposure.

"Probably the most devastating damage that can be done to the human psyche by improper uses of the sexual process involves childhood rape and incest. The psychological implantations branch out into one's relationship with the entire human race, the human subconscious protective system operating as it does. Therefore, proper treatment is urged, to make the best use of the lifetime and relationships following the incident.

"Present-life male lust is usually responsible for most aberrant social and marital responses, regardless of past-life carryovers. A proper release IS available, plus understanding and treatment via a meaningful therapy. What was thought to be a secret encounter is harbored by the soul, and festers in predictable ways seldom witnessed by the perpetrator of the aberrant behavior. Is that clear?

"You are encouraged to investigate the subject further for yourself by asking for guidance and greater light, more understanding, leading to that "Peace Which Passeth All Understanding."

"We hope and trust we have cleared things up a bit.

"We rest."

[Editor: Please consult the Suggested Reading Section]

CHAPTER 13

The Psychic Sexual Apparatus

"Already apparent and well accepted is the fact that there is little enough curiosity regarding the true nature and availability of the human psychic sexual machinery. We shall not belabor you with repetition of already well-known factors which in themselves control or at least influence the quality of one's sexual performance which can be anticipated and experienced reqularly, once aroused, when said apparatus is kept in fine working condition, maintained and used properly.

"Less well known is the effect which mental and more subtle factors have on both the male and the female ability to perform satisfactorily sexually on demand. Those certain subjective factors are in themselves more heavily dependent upon mental *and* spiritual conditioning, more on thoughts and feelings, on appearances, than they are on the so-called *facts* of physical or economic conditions. And most of all, it is but little realized how dependent in turn both the mind *and* the physical factors are upon dietary and body chemistry factors as yet but little accepted or controlled by the general public.

"Not yet of general public interest, the subject of PSYCHIC SEX is indeed about to be aired, brought into a life of its own, for the relatively simple reason that soon enough the world scene will shift dramatically, enough so that one's selection of foods available to be eaten will become very limited. Once it becomes difficult or outright impossible to obtain much of the processed foods, those few persons who acclimate to survival eating will find that there is a restoration of mental acuity and physical libido, with attendant increase in birth rates as a minimum result of having minimal chemical pollutants present in the foods and liquids consumed, especially noteworthy among the more intellectually oriented peoples.

"We are declaring that as soon as humans revert to a fundamentally quiet, pure, undamaged diet, made up of mostly the raw natural foods and edibles, it will be discovered that their sexual activity is bound to improve in quality, if not in frequency, the bodies then operating as originally intended.

"We have just told you that the proper foods taken into the flesh permit restoration of major amounts of original activity. The observed decline in Caucasian male sexuality is not experienced in other cultures or races, and need not be experienced. We report additionally that it need not be necessary to wait until physical calamity befall the planet for a person to restore and regain use of his or her sexual apparatus.

"Consider the implications that there are subtle energy flows on several levels of the human as a composite and completed design. Nerve trunks and networks already are understood to unite Mind and Flesh, but the part played by the invisible or indiscernible spiritual nature of Thought is hardly recognized, let alone properly considered. When the actuality of Thought-Energy flows on all three lower levels is recognized and properly nurtured, one becomes able to assure herself or himself of undiminished sexual vigor on the higher levels of activity all one's incarnate days.

"There are indeed several ways to restore most of one's sexual performance. A high tone of physical conditioning enables a person to take in the larger amounts of Oxygen needed to keep the inner fires burning, so that larger amounts of Adrenaline are available to stir the physical structures to their highest rate of energy consumption, i.e., to assure efficient carburetion. In turn, once the greater oxygen consumption is restored, the heart muscles can again pump the required amounts of blood flow to assure tumescence of the respective male and female sexual apparatus.

"And of course, there is also the factor of mental ATTITUDE. Because of the primary role attitude plays in the associated mental current flow processes, the place and power of the mind to influence the relative efficiency of one's sexual performance cannot go unnoticed.

"Here we again note that the subtler influences operating in one's overall ability or interest in functioning sexually are experienced on three discernible levels. Then, rather than just being between the legs, proper and full access to the heights of sexual enjoyment requires proper conditioning and balancing on each level for the spiritual currents, the Prana, the Kundalini, to integrate and energize each corresponding activity on each and on all three of those levels. We note again, from yet another point of view, that without said properly integrated and balanced current flows, it is impossible for a human couple to experience the heights and delights which the Tantra devotee and couple can experience.

"Of course, the human race will make do, accepting whatever forms and degrees of sexual expression are at hand to enjoy. However, it is almost always feasible for copulating couples to further heighten their sexual experience by PROPER EXERCISE, PROPER EATING HABITS, PROPER THINKING, and PROPER ENVIRONMENTAL FACTORS.

"When it comes down to putting on the finishing touches, one needs to be freed of mental patterns, free of recorded programming which usually controls what its autonomous ego-defense and control system permits to influence the sexual processes. When a person has recordings of taboos and trauma connected with sexual activities, it becomes difficult or impossible for the person to experience energy flows strong enough to guarantee a useful erection in the male, or a corresponding orgasmic condition in the female.

"We are telling you that the condition of the subconscious mind, with all its programming operating constantly without conscious direction or detection, is a larger single factor in human sexual performance and pleasure than any other, excepting actual surgical or physiological damage to the associated neural communication lines.

"Anyone who would prepare himself to experience only and always the highest levels of sexual enjoyment will do well to commence an in-depth program of self-discovery to renew, update and remedy the sex-related processes and recordings operating from below the level of awareness.

"Subconscious recordings at all related to trauma, violation, feelings of inadequacy in any portion of the human psyche, or inhibitions from family or cultural sources, guilt, fears of discovery or pregnancy or disease . . . all are probably still operating to reduce one's freedom to be a sexual being. Inhibitions from past-lives are carried forward—even religious vows taken in earlier incarnations often are still influencing the returned incarnate soul.

"When intercourse is attempted under inhibitive or otherwise unsatisfactory conditions, the higher sensibilities are reduced or note operating, sometimes preventing copulation at all, except when one partner (usually the male) is compulsively driven to perform the act. The human race will survive as long as the human male is susceptible to forces liberated by a desirous female, almost regardless of other conditions at the time. Then perhaps the LAST thing the spiritual aspirant need consider is whether the human race will cease to exist because of his or her personal celibacy.

"Given that maintenance of world population is removed as a problem for consideration here, we can move forward to considering how a person can magnify his and her enjoyment of the already-available sexual joys.

"We summarize our position at the moment as requiring three factors to be properly opened and balanced, so that the human reproductive processes shall be available in their highest working condition for enjoyment, as contrasted to only enough libido to reproduce.

"Let it be recognized that there is a hidden payoff for having undertaken to provide one's sexual expressions at the very highest levels of mutual enjoyment . . . transcending the satisfactions of lust, however enticing. The greatest spiritualized enjoyment produces or attracts only the highest levels of spirit beings into incarnation. When undertaken for the purposes of both recreation *and* reproduction, the waves of Spirit radiate through neighborhood galactic space, as if advertising that an opportunity to incarnate is being generated, so that interested candidates can consider themselves being solicited.

"One might suspect that *any* involvement of drugs into the sexual processes would have direct or indirect effects on one's capacity for and ability to enjoy himself. Use of contraceptive methods also can improve or lessen the enjoyment capable of being experienced. When several contraceptive methods are employed simultaneously, the heights of available enjoyment are diminished, to be sure, even if some participating couples are unwilling or unable to enjoy sexuality without them! Perhaps having a little pleasure is better than having none at all, but the long-term effects should at least be considered.

"For example, let it be contemplated that use of the simple basic condom by design serves well to retain the male fluids, and at times diminishing the possibility of disease transfer from one partner to the other. But at the same time, it is observable clairvoyantly that lessened current flows also are operating to reduce the intensity of the kundalini force, making sexual intercourse a less pleasurable thing.

"Other chemical products widely known to be capable of preventing pregnancy and initiating abortion are available in the USA and France. As with 'the Pill' in the times this discourse is being prepared (1988), all are widely used. Many users throw caution to the winds when 'On the Pill,' but the fear of pregnancy is subordinated to other fears, such as guilt, the exercise of propriety, the operation of ingrained social or religious factors. These in turn directly relate to the accepted inner-self programming operating at the time of a sexual liaison or union.

"Stimulants taken to enhance sexual performance are known to be available, but almost always are attended with complicating factors. Certain members of the herbal Cannabis family (from which we derive the expression 'connubial bliss') are known to gorge the sexual areas with blood, to promote tumescence, but the user risks uncontrollable hemorrhaging. What constitutes excess differs widely from one person to the next. It is more or less obvious that age, or decrepitating bodies, out of condition, sated with alcohol or other mind-deadening fluids and foods, serve to impair one's capacity even for simple love-making, enjoyment . . . recreational use of the human sexual equipment, and deny access to the higher sensate levels.

"Then it appears that one's highest enjoyment of the god-given capacity to use sexual activity for pleasure is *heavily dependent*, not only on subtle current flows, but also on how well one observes other subjective factors, such as the Social Mores of the times, on psychological, physiological an biological factors, and/or on one's relative responsiveness to the subtler wavelengths of the human soul and mind.

"The fact that subjective factors are operating is often noted when one person feels some inner revulsion or attraction to another person. Subtle past-life factors may or may not be operating to encourage or to prevent sexual activity, because the same feelings can be generated from one's unconscious programming, but the disgust or attraction factor is removed or honored in different ways.

"When a person has begun consciously to prepare for reception of the higher forces or energies, the real spiritual energies, he becomes sensitized to those same lesser-evident forces operating in other persons, in addition to his own. He gradually becomes susceptible to the IDEA that subtle sexual forces are operating, which are often interpretations of a more fundamental nature than a psychic affinity. Then, rather than God telling a couple to copulate, it is entirely probable that some old chemical or programmed Akashic condition is stirring up unrecognized sources. Too often the presence or operation of Love is entirely absent!

"The human ego-self is almost wildly creative in finding excuses for, and in arranging ways to do what it wants to do, or in finding excuses for NOT doing same. Hence, when a person claims that 'God wants me to do this,' or that 'the Devil made me do it,' it is often interesting and well to look deeper into the root cause for one's urges to manifest sexually.

"There are indeed discarnate forces operating in the universe, most often humans who died without having ever really satisfied themselves in the sexual aspects of incarnate life. They are still seeking conditions and receptive or controllable humans to do FOR them and THROUGH them what they are unable to do without having flesh of their own. Simply stated, this means that spiritual possession may be present and operating, as when persons indulge in drugs, alcohol, and sexual orgies. Persons in orgiastic situations thus contribute to their own later discarnate dissatisfactions, and ultimately are required by the ongoing-ness of Life Itself to relieve themselves of such driving forces.

"The deeper is one's participation in orgiastic activity, the more lifetimes are required to release said soul from entrapment to such addictive activity. Such activity is perpetuated through reincarnation until the urgency burns itself out. Basically degenerative in nature, such souls draw or relegate themselves into later or following lifewaves. If pursued to the usual end, one can confine self to the Eternal Darkness, the 'outer darkness' of the Bible.

"At this point we hope and trust that we have made our points strongly enough and clearly enough so we have shown that you CAN and MAY enhance your own sexual intercommunication activities. We have at least exposed you to the processes at work in the human so that you will strive to perfect yourself in Diet, in Thought, in Physical Exercise, and in use of the Spoken Word to manifest condi-tions of a mutually satisfactory nature, and that one must indeed prepare himself and herself for living in and enjoying life on ALL LEVELS . . . simultaneously!

"Perhaps you are beginning to cognize that sexual relations on the higher levels have hardly been thought about, in the rush to go out and 'get laid.'

"Now, let it be additionally recognized that there comes a time when the human will not need sexual intercourse, either to create additional forms for incoming spirit, or for expression of the highest possible affinities. It is indeed possible, and has been demonstrated in present-life circumstances (by persons known to the author) that it is possible for a higher level of affinity to be expressed WITHOUT THE USE OF HUMAN SEXUAL ORGANS. It becomes a matter then of learning to differentiate between what is known and practiced as PERSONAL LOVE versus what is called TRANSPERSONAL or simply as IMPERSONAL LOVE . . . love without physical sex as known and often practiced on Earth."

A MEDITATION ON SEXUALITY

"The higher spiritual current flows become sensible most readily to persons in the higher levels of mental and/or intellectual development, and certainly are well known to be more an intuitive factor. However, access to the higher spiritual currents becomes available to any persons who practice and more or less perfect their mental-spiritual contacts with the Energy of Life through meditation.

"By developing skills in focusing one's mind through meditation and contemplation, one becomes aware of how to make us of the subtle creative forces which permeate the Universe . . . without which Life as humans know it would not exist.

"Then, if you would increase your capacity for experiencing higher levels of Life, JOY TRANSCENDENT, you can do no better than to undertake sincere study of *both* the theory *and* the practice of Meditation on the Life currents.

"Improper development of the Kundalini energy flows has damaged human flesh, and indeed it is possible to become so unbalanced as to endanger one's sanity. However, with most advanced students of Life, unbalanced development is unlikely. The Master or Teacher imparts a certain amount of self-regulation, by which the true in-depth student backs off from overdoing exercises which are capable of delaying or ruining his or her optimal spiritual development.

"HOWEVER, it is also true that many presently incarnate persons are intent on *leaving* the planet. They try to accomplish their goal by MISUSE of the kundalini forces through use of alcohol and drugs. They indeed make contact with other states of consciousness, often irrevocably so, but risk permanent damage to their etheric vehicles for nearly All-Time. One is most likely to find a proper method of spiritual development through meditation in schools like the Self Realization Fellowship, and the Unity School of Christianity, The Arcane School, and there be others. Advanced students are led to work directly with their own personal Guide(s), where individual attention is given to one's overall balanced development.

"We shall wind down this morning by summarizing our previous points.

"We have introduced several concepts of what is required to become both proficient and popular in expressing one's feeling-self sexually. We have shown that there is a combination of factors which work to enhance or to work against one's ability to enjoy himself or herself to the highest possible degree. With having brought those factors to mind, let it be incumbent upon the reader to seek out ways to unburden self of unnecessary hindrances to expressing the sexual life more normally. For having done so, it will be found that Life OVERALL is enhanced greatly . . . WITH or WITHOUT use of the gonads.

"One final factor to be considered is that the conventional 'Adam and Eve' or 'missionary style' of intercourse, making use of supine positions, in which the female is superimposed with the male body, head-to-head and toe-to-toe has a fundamentally good thing going for it. In that position it will be understood that the Spiritual Centers are correctly aligned, so that the male and female current flows are able to correspond one-for-one. The female energies and the male energies, in the literal Yin and Yang sense, are balanced, are best able to become balanced. When the centers are cleared of debris, the maximal amounts of current can flow, thus heightening the mutual enjoyment, the Oneness in Spirit of both parties. In the truest sense of the word, male and female alike again become united as one flesh...united in the highest manner possible to physically incarnate human souls, physically, mentally,and spiritually.

"We have held our preceding point to the end of this discourse so you will retain the message that your OWN highest enjoyment of the sexual process depends greatly and almost entirely upon having removed all that blocks your expression as Spirit in Flesh. That it has always been thus is seldom recognized. It is Man's OWN FAULT that he and she have seldom experienced the tantric levels of sexual enjoyment enroute to Heaven.

"Stated yet one more time, Man's use of the Creative Energies is almost always experienced through he gonads, through the orgasm producing portions of the reproductive organs. If there were no orgasmic potentials for human pleasure, it is unlikely that Man would be better off than the animals which he looks down upon. THEY use the creative function *as intended*. Man has been unwilling to develop himself beyond the point where HE TOO would use sexual intercourse only for procreation.

"Then, if YOU would enhance and perfect YOUR sexuality,

experiencing it on tantric and the higher spiritual levels, you clearly may do so at your own elected pace, time, and place. When a person seeks to perfect his sexual nature, he will find himself necessarily perfecting himself on ALL LEVELS.

"Quoting William Shakespeare . . . 'Aye, there's the rub!' Man is forever directly responsible for his OWN condition in life, and not the least of those considerations is his or own ATTITUDES and conditions of mind and body and soul. Best, then, that he and she attend once again to his and her own self-mastery, no longer being controlled by sexuality.

"Some people say that everything reminds them of sex. But to us, Sex reminds US of *Life* and of its polarities operating in balanced overall patterns, which in itself produces JOY TRANSCENDENT.

"If you want the BEST THERE IS, it is necessary to PERFECT YOURSELF, to be able to receive it and share it on all levels.

"OK?"

CHAPTER

14

The Creative Process In Reverse

"Before we start anew to commence another project, we first undertake to assess the market for the product. Whenever we shall note that it is worthy of putting ourselves to the task of finding an Earthplanes outlet and getting same up to speed, we ourselves often need to find a channel, an outlet, a transcriber well-enough indoctrinated, one who is willing to put up with all the personal inconvenience of said preparation and service. We thusly assure ourselves that we shall then have no difficulty with persistence, with follow-through, with completion of said project, before we commit either ourselves or the resources and services of the willing Earth terminal. We then are not always assured of success, or are we always minded to begin, just because we have once previously undertaken a successful earlier project with a use of a particular channel, even if the project is perhaps of similar or identical content or message.

"This morning we have undertaken another chapter to be included within the intended limits of this book on human sexuality as witnessed form the higher vantage point we enjoy. Having now begun, we shall eagerly anticipate its completion in one sitting. We shall then undertake sending the manuscript through to the publishers and distributors, then into the hands of that ever-hungry vacuum of the human mind, filling up the hunger of the Human Race for advantageous position with regards living an Earthlife successfully. That process is both a challenge and as well an opportunity, for without having an illumined populace from which to draw our Through-The-Veil Recruits, we find ourselves as if shunted off into a mysterious cavern, relegated into a nonexistent and legendary sort of heaven which has little or no validity at all to the incarnate human race.

"A few members of said human race, having made frequent enough forays into the Great Beyond, are able to convince enough others among themselves so that there is an undercurrent of belief that a greater good exists, somewhere, such that it is worthy of enjoining a search for said secret or hidden passageway into said heaven kingdom. Then, whether or not said secret passageway may be found has been deemed by humanity-at-large as worthy of devoting some considerable effort as to its attainment, as possession of that mystery is given value beyond the things of Earth.

"Whenever another person becomes convinced of the reality and availability of that secret life, of that Heaven-on-Earth, enough so that he or she becomes willing to make significant changes in his or her manner of living, we observe whether said revisions effect what is entertained as giving pleasure. Necessary change is usually found to alleviate or even on occasion, to eliminate abuse of the human flesh, even to eliminate or to modify or greatly revise one's lifelong habits and pursuits for attainment of or for qualification of some invisible condition somewhere in the Beyond, significantly marks said personage as perhaps demented, or at least as being misguide . . . however well intentioned. Having undertaken so to modify one's traditional living patterns then marks many of such converts as being some sort of nut, if not an outright fool.

"For us then successfully to sell our wares, to convince people who are still wearing the flesh of Earthlife, is to overcome some very strong forces. We Guides tend always to be identified as quasi-existent, nobody really being certain that we do or do not have beingness. We usually lack enough conviction to the usual Earthling, such that if we cannot produce an immediate effect, a miracle of one sort or another, we are assessed to be of little use, as if we did not exist at all.

"Then finding ways to express our realness, to validate our total existence, is perhaps the most difficult thing we have to do. It becomes one thing to find ourselves a willing transcriber, a channel though the veil, but quite yet another thing to find enough willing customers such that we can launch into a successful campaign of selling both our ideas and enlisting their services. We then readily recognize the difficulty in overcoming Inertia, Disdain, and outright Hostility as we attempt to forge and perhaps to force our ways into the mental and physical lives of enough incarnate Earth persons to make the venture worth undergoing all the associated stresses and uncertainties intrinsic to self-christing.

"Perhaps immediately you cognize on some facet of our existence as a provable factor in the lives of persons who have tried working with us, having done so with enough success to demonstrate that by whatever form we had done so, our influence has been made demonstrable through modification of said personal changes successfully made to life patterns which were upset, seemingly so that significant changes COULD be produced, and *were*.

"By operating at first almost entirely ON FAITH in our presence, our subsequent viability can surely be considered as having adequately been proved. There should then be no further need for us to belabor whether we have reality or not, sufficient then to have demonstrated ourselves and our ability to make truly significant gains in the lives of enough incarnate souls so that we shall bypass the usual introductory proof-of-existence processes and launch directly into examination of certain unseen or unrecognized portions of the overall creative processes of Life itself.

"We have titled this chapter "The Creative Process in Reverse" as if to initiate a reexamination of certain forces which are found to UNDO or reduce one's capacity to live a life in happiness and abundance. Unless and until one has thoroughly taken to heart to investigate our offered allegation that Life *can* be lived progressively, neutrally, or regressively, one cannot be expected to accomplish any permanent changes of significance in himself. For having undertaken personal investigation and proof of our offered approaches, the candidate will surely find merit in making great sacrifices, thusly averting loss of one's health, and will sacrifice certain forms of relationship which delay and interfere with prevent obtaining one's overall highest available good.

"Whenever we are able to reach the minds of suitably responsive humans, we can often show clearly which uses of the Creative Process in reverse need be discontinued or modified, to cease being destructive. We can show which practices and forces will be found constructive, perhaps requiring another avenue of living, in successfully modifying one's life patterns as to bring spiritual growth and fulfillment. We can quickly demonstrate that meaningful sacrifice of some of what makes life seem worthwhile produces successful co-workers, successful practitioners. Much of what is sought traditionally is then abandoned by persons who have applied the Creative Process in reverse all too successfully, degeneratively.

"One can surely recognize that most of Humanity is engaged in REVERSE application of the same processes which ordinarily would ENHANCE life and livingness, if used sparingly. One task is then surely to provide the comparisons by which it will become readily evident that PROPER and SUSTAINED APPLICATION of certain easy but unglamorous processes of life expression, like correct eating, are more satisfactorily applied over a life span than merely to live a life of least resistance, taking whatever forms of pleasure become available, and accepting the consequences.

"And even that latter approach could be considered acceptable, were a person's approach to suffer avoidance of excessive use of any particular aspect or form of life expression. This has to do with the AMOUNTS and TYPES of undertaking, and surely is recognized to include excesses which have been shown to damage the human capacity for Life Expression. We naturally include sexuality, hedonistic overeating and toxicities, and inflicting pain on others for the feelings of power and superiority it seems to give the inflictor.

"Perhaps it is worthy to consider that The Creative Process is complete, and that it can be applied in either of two ways. The creative Process can generate a short-term sense of well-being in one's current affairs. If correctly applied over the longer-term, it produces feelings of well-being both in Mind *and* Body. This amounts to suggesting that one can reap his or her rewards at a faster rate but risk burnout, or can take it easy and spread out that wonderful process over an entire lifetime, living conservatively, then never needing to sacrifice anything except perhaps a lessened susceptibility to enjoy life at all.

"We make the point that unless destructive processes are minimized or eliminated entirely, the human soul and body-mind cannot enjoy Life as fully as it was and is given him. Beyond the initial discovery, if then not followed by self-exploitation and experiencing permanent damage, with diminishing ability to participate, one is free to indulge in Creativity at whatever level is or was originally sought at the time of embodiment.

"We are already aware of our ability, of our potential for overstating the obvious when we claim that it is easily possible to try doing . . . overdoing anything, especially when it comes to the misuses or overuses of food, sexuality, drugs, and/or use of pain for pleasure-seeking purposes.

"Then perhaps one still needs to listen to us for another few pages, to allow us to complete our case, presenting ourselves as possessing HIGHER FORMS of pain-pleasure than you are likely to discover *for* yourself or *by* yourself, without undergoing a considerable degree of intensive well-directed study and cleansing.

"It is no longer necessary for a human soul incarnate on Earth to make the trek through Time and Space unaided. Guideposts are abundantly to be found along the way, for he and she who are able to spare enough attention to perceive them. Looking then for subtleties, acknowledging the finer essences of both mind and body, is perhaps the most immediately available manner of finding that Higher Life to which the classical search is oriented. We then are suggesting, even while undergoing investigation of pleasure-producing processes, that one take the time and make the effort at discovering that there are several identifiable degrees of enjoyment.

"Were it not so, how could one person go into raptures over a beautiful sunset or a painting, over the delicate fragrance of a flower, or even in a cup of tea. Or how could a person respond so innocently to voiced or projected thoughts of love and acceptance experienced in or from another person? How could a person participate in exploration of the more delicate currents of the human spirit as they weave in and out of the thoughts and spiritual essences of the disembodied human soul, if they were not discernible?

"What if there were no persons who could sense those exquisite essences of Life, no one who could produce similar effects in other willing candidates? Perhaps we would then be without a point, would be then wasting both time and opportunity trying to spread the news, the gospel of our presence, and hence of the presence and existence of a whole parallel universe of Joy even within and surrounding you.

"We are investing the necessary effort at applying our available resources, including the willing support of our transcriber's Time and Material. We have the firm goal of informing the willing reader that THERE IS INDEED a PARALLEL UNIVERSE in which anyone can function who makes the effort at becoming sensitized to it.

"Ask the drug addicts to tell you of their finding in the special world of the senses, in which everything is all-glorious, if you would seek stark and often hideous evidence of the existence of that portion of the mental universe. We do have one thing in common with such personages . . . we too are aware of their findings, but with one exception. WE DO NOT NEED DRUGS TO GAIN ENTRY INTO THE HIGHER ASPECTS OF THAT SPECIAL KINGDOM OF THE SENSES, and WE have no hangovers. We experience only the Beauty!

"That Special Kingdom is *approachable* via Tantra Yoga, and *available* by direct efforts at Self Christing. To distinguish some of the subtle differences between those two approaches to The Kingdom of Permanent Pleasure, let us begin by stating clearly that there is NO ADDICTION required to experience them, if one approaches them correctly. By either approach, it is NOT NECESSARY to destroy or damage a human body or mind. If anything stands out to differentiate between OUR approach and classical Judeo-Christianity is that Tantra may attract remnants of what you see in the bars and drug palaces, or in the brothels and gaming rooms. Our approach results in rising above those lower attractions, while enhancing one's ability to express Life on ALL LEVELS SIMULTANEOUSLY. OUR addicts no longer are enticed by the lower 'vibes,' and are most likely to be found enjoying robust health, much more so than most so-called normal or typical incarnate Earth-lings.

"Then indeed, the Creative Process CAN BE APPLIED IN RE-VERSE, or in the intended FORWARD or Evolutional direction. What one makes of his or her life lies almost entirely in the manner chosen for applying the Laws of Creativity, and to what ends they are applied. The most direct approach is to LIVE and OBSERVE CON-SERVATIVELY all the patterns and experiences of incarnate life, so that one misses nothing of value along the way, and neither dulls nor overlooks senses capable of producing joy."

ADDENDUM

"Part of the purpose of this chapter is to announce that the observed process of deterioration of the human mind and flesh is due almost entirely to MISUSE or to OVERUSE of the Creative Processes . . . to their use in the reverse or negative directions, then causing or accelerating deterioration or disassembly from what should ordinarily be considered as CREATIVE or CONSTRUCTIVE applications of that Divine Law. In other words, overdoing a good thing often leads to unwanted or unanticipated results

"Sometimes in the search for happiness, when one seems unable to achieve his desires and goals through normal relationships with other people and with the world, a temporary sense of well-being IS obtainable through over-stimulation of normal body experiences, for the length of time required to desensitize the sensory protective mechanisms. Usually the dose size increases for a desired result, leading to addiction, and then to failure to find peace or satisfaction at any dose level.

"A definition of CONSTRUCTIVE or CREATIVE processes is then 'that which promotes the normal processes of the human experience to achieve a sense of well-being on all levels.'

"That which causes destruction or diminution of human sensory processes of any ilk,, and their mechanisms, is here considered a REVERSE APPLICATION, and hence becomes a subject of this dissertation."

15

How Good Can It Get?

"During sexual intercourse of whatever type and on whatever levels experienced, there are unsensed subjective or psychic energy flows. The intensity of the energy flow corresponds to the overall states of mind and body of each party to the act. For ideal sexual intercourse to be experienced, it is fundamentally necessary that each party to the interchange, to the mutual congress, shall have no barriers, that their chakras are cleared, aligned properly, and rotating at approximately the same frequencies. In other words, the participants should be in excellent or perfect health, and experience affinity on all seven levels of human beingness.

"Identifying conditions needing correction for perfection of the self merits investigation, and of itself is sufficient cause for producing this text. One can assess in advance his capabilities and/or qualifications to experience 'all there is' by scrutinizing his and her relationships during his or her normal daytime experience. If there be unresolved fear, anger or hate, guilt, if there be withholding, if there be psychological factors mitigating against expression of feelings, it is unlikely that either Personal Love *or* Impersonal Love can be expressed richly, or that Impersonal Love can be recognized, if experienced at all. Not until one has 'cleared up his case' can the concept of Perfect Sex be experienced . . . or even GOOD sex: it must remain just that . . . a concept.

"The Ancients developed the arts of living to perfection in the various branches of Yoga. Perhaps most familiar will be the Asanas of Hatha Yoga, exercises for body health. When the teachings were mastered, the student-practitioner was reunited with God. In fact, the word 'yoga' itself holds connotations of 'yoke' or 'union.'

"Kriya Yoga has been popularized and made available by Paramhansa Yogananda as a direct method for attaining God Consciousness. For the persons who would achieve perfect union with the godness in each other through sexuality, Tantra Yoga is recommended as an attainable step for many seekers. Several excellent references are listed in the Bibliography.

"Today's swing of the Great Pendulum dictates social usage and mores, teaching that it is the male who is supposed to instruct the female about sexuality, leading her to fulfillment. It was not always thus! In the ancient temples, the Priestesses, among their other duties, initiated males into the higher forms of sexual intercourse, of its practice and abstract or spiritual qualities. Their ancient arts need not be lost to the serious student of Tantra Yoga. However, it takes a lot of digging to find those secrets in the literature, and few persons would be able to heed the instructions even if offered at firsthand. A certain amount of psychic and spiritual training and responsiveness must be developed first, else the candidate will be unable to gain much from the exercises.

"First among the things to be done is to clear the candidate's subconscious mind of blocks and barriers to gain access to and permit free expression of the human soul. That freedom includes release from psychological barriers, any antisocial or other inappropriate program-ming, bad habits, poor attitudes, insensitivities to the subtle thoughts and feelings of one's partner, and ignorance of the Life Forces. These factors each and all prevent an incarnate spirit from sharing its own life with the lives of companions similarly incarnate in flesh.

"Consider that a female and a male each have seven major chakras, although there are many more lesser centers. Let us label the first chakra as the sexual or root center. In both sexes, that center is at the root of the spine, and is said to guard the sacred fires of Kundalini.

"Life energy entering the human solar plexus is distributed throughout the psychic pathways, energizing the entire chakra-nerve system of the mind-body complex, to the extent they are unblocked [read Leadbeater]. During intercourse, the male receives and diverts Life energy to the root center, awakening the Kundalini force, from which it flows into the female chakra system during the sex act, peaking at orgasm. While the resulting satisfaction permeates the male genital area, it is perceived in the mind. However, were the male able to raise that same energy consciously to the higher centers, as can most females, even if unknowingly, much greater mutual satisfaction would be experienced.

"Females are traditionally and often much more receptive than males to the subtle feelings (currents) of love than males. Females of all races are more responsive to feelings through their Heart Center, so that for the female, the sex experience is apt to be richer than it is for the male, even without experience of orgasm.

"Now, females can be taught how to visualize and to FEEL those currents. They can be taught to direct the Life Energy (the Kundalini currents) to flow from their heart down into their own first center, through the vagina and penis over into the male first center at the base of his spine, up into his own heart chakra, and hence returning back into her heart center. That tantric process is available to most humans for sexual application, without regards to their higher degrees of spiritual attainment. Actual orgasm is then not at all necessary to attain the heightened senses and Bliss beyond the traditional simultaneous orgasm. Without orgasm, those delights can be maintained for hours at a time, as the two persons enjoy sending and receiving Life Energy through each other.

"For persons willing to develop further their spirituality, to enhance the receptivity and sensitivity of the heart, throat, brow, and crown chakras, a higher level of bliss becomes available, transcending what can be told in words."Being One with God" is about all you can call it, and is the Eternal Bliss of which the ancients and masters of all times tell, the Impersonal Love which they and the Christed Ones have achieved.

"When a female and her male have developed their higher centers, the centers above the belt, to the point of sensing and directing the energy flows, they can continue the above processes by sending and sensing the kundalini currents up through into the throat and the brow and the crown chakras. It is then returned down the right side of the spine of the male partner, to be sent across into the female body and up the left side of her spine. The participants are permitted to try sending the currents in the opposite directions, determining for themselves that they have reached the ultimate bliss. The two souls become as one; a higher union is unavailable to incarnate humanity.

"Enroute to that ideal state or condition, when the higher centers are more or less asleep or inactive, when the lower chakras are spinning idly, operating only partially, some fundamental or elementary but satisfying sufficient level of ecstasy can be approached. This is a normal state of affairs for most of contemporary human civilization. However, we can safely announce that you can do much better than that for learning what you are doing!

"Interestingly enough, it is unnecessary to have a human body of the opposite sex present to experience the orgasm process. The human mind is able to make mental mock-ups, to visualize, imagine or fantasize an exciting companion, perhaps an actor or an athlete, perhaps infrequently the Presence of God.

"Biblically it is said that to contemplate, to fantasize, a sexual union with another is equal to having performed same in flesh. To us that condition is neither good nor bad, but it does underline the veracity of our statement. Then ideally, one approximates making self One With All Life according to his or her level of realized spiritualization. Under the highest of such conditions, physical orgasm may be found disruptive, gross, unless done in a sacrificial manner for procreation.

"To jump into bed with a book in one hand and your partner in the other, with your attention focussed intellectually somewhere in between, is to miss most of what a spontaneous sexual relationship is all about. Spontaneity is essential. We trust you readily see that mere procreation, by design, can take place even under the worst of conditions, whereas high Love instead calls for the best available circumstances!

"Preliminaries for suggesting, preparing for, approaching, and experiencing the higher states of sexuality include the conscious use of touch, whether of hands or lips, or a gentle hug, because of the energy interchange which can occur. Spontaneous exchange of affinity may thus be offered and received. Even the touch of a hand to a shoulder, or two finger tips making contact can hold high significance to attuned parties.

"On the basic physical levels, an overall body massage done under loving conditions can be an overall caress, and is capable of providing a highly satisfying form of intercourse, even if orgasm is neither sought nor reached. Unless otherwise taboo, almost any sort of gentle but respectful caress exchanged is then permitted, subject to avoiding damage to the delicate human tissues, or to a sensitive psyche, or avoiding affronts to the dignity of the human soul and social mores.

"Inflicting pain by any of the forms of bestiality is found absolutely unnecessary, devoid of Love, and counterproductive even to the lowest forms of sexual expression. Sadomasochistic misuse dulls and nulls and voids the higher qualities of the experience, leaving said practitioners incapable of matching what can be obtained from having prepared one's soul of self on *any* higher level.

"We then have discussed four distinct levels of sexual expression; using the lower center only, using the three centers below the belt, adding or using the higher centers above the belt, and, employing them all. Ideally, both the lower and the upper centers will be active and matched, balanced among themselves, and balanced between the partners. For the most advanced partners, use of the three lower chakras is not at all necessary. That kind of Love can be experienced without flesh, as in the after-death state. Except for deliberate procreation, to cause pregnancy, use or experience of physical orgasm is not necessary.

"In other words, homosexuality is not considered here as capable of providing the polarities necessary for perfect balancing of the spiritual currents made possibly by conventional "missionary style" male-female sexual intercourse, i.e., wherein male and female are superimposed in each other's embrace, face to face, center to center.

"Surely it will be recognized even in the sexual relationship, that perfection is no trifle, but that trifles lead to perfection expressed!

"Ye verily, AS ABOVE, SO BELOW!"

16

Tips To Tantric Union

"A few basic positions are used almost universally for human sexual intercourse. Many sophisticated variations have been developed, making that gentle practice an art form, practiced professionally, and as well internally to the privacy of one's own domicile. These facts should bring no great gasps of surprise. Had we told you otherwise, you would have reason to doubt our credibility, beyond the basic fact that endemic to human life there is but one basic design each for male and female bodies. Man has become ingenious in his ways to prolong the sexual act, being limited by the more or less obvious fact that the bodies and minds of All Mankind are still built to the same fundamental specifications.

"The fact that the male organ points downward to the center of Mother Earth in the elementary sex act is of itself significant, for it was intended that Gravity should enhance the flow of the seminal fluids which contain the reproductive sperm, thus to reach the intended ovum in quantity. We then consider that there is really only one natural way properly to assure the sexual processes necessary to fulfill the intended purpose of reproduction. Then, anything else, any other form of using the human body for pleasure has originated in the collective Mind of Man.

"Consider a popular battle flag carried by Japanese soldiers in World War II. It was about one meter square, of light blue silk, and displayed drawings of the famed One Hundred Positions for sexual engagement. Within them there are apt to be shades of duplication, but the objective of issuing such a flag was to keep morale high. Providing their troops with such a symbol of victory over the weaker female sex was surely one factor in exciting the Japanese soldier with the passions to conquer his American enemy. Of course, the American GI also had his pin-ups!

"When it comes to researching and documenting additional approaches to gaining pleasure from the human sexual apparatus, the Hindus cannot be gainsaid, cannot be found wanting. In ages past, they too had produced scores of challenging positions, documenting them in statuary at Ankor Wat. Dedicated by the kings and priests of ancient origin, they were set up to assure fertility among their populace, and at the same time to assure public entertainment through offering demonstrations of new techniques and forms of sexual expression. Their tradesmen brought home and sold new ideas as they returned from their foreign travels. Enhancement of sexual creativity in that era was highly rewarded, and produced the lucrative trade in spices used as aphrodisiacs.

"As you readily begin to appreciate, Dear Reader, you are unlikely to see much competition develop in *these* days from what we ourselves did, as the Ancients, when compared to the voluminous research taken by Man in our *previous* incarnations, in earlier decades, centuries, and ages. Then, as now, much of such activity originated in seeking release from boredom, from overuse and satiation of the formerly sacred sexual reproductive function.

"Any time a person or race gets to the point where he has little else to do physically or mentally as when institutionalized, or when a living is easily made, one invariably reverts to sensual overindulgence. This is usually accompanied or followed by overeating, becoming sated with exotic foods and drinking to excess. When these approaches fail to produce the desired highs, use of aphrodisiacs and drugs is attempted, until nothing remains except bestiality, and even that ultimately fails.

"One thus can take ones's physiological and psychological pulse, can discern his or her own spiritual development status, by observing the methods he or she takes to provide self with amusement and/or pleasure.

"In that simple test, we are able to offer Humanity an excellent yardstick for measuring itself. In that naive-seeming sentence/concept are contained the factors of appetite indulgence in the face of not needing to eat at all beyond body needs, beyond eating only enough to maintain robust and resilient health. Perhaps gluttony, when available, is then the second most used means whereby mankind can strive for satisfaction, as when the human mind, soul, or body becomes sated and no longer can respond adequately to the available sexual processes. This is particularly true with males, but by no means is limited thereto, as when the female is unable to attract a male. The appetite for exotic foods is one of the last appetites to go: food almost always tastes good, at any age.

"Another perhaps more widely distributed variation of the heterosexual process will be found to include simple masturbation. It too can take on many forms and fetishes, each intended to produce interim satisfaction for the user of that ancient approach to self-indulgence. And of course, there is little to add here to the vast arrays of man-made substitute devices to counterfeit and to simulate the organs of the opposite sex.

"Self-relief offers the classical potential for sailors and soldiers, prisoners and other isolated humans, persons on long journeys, wherein the various members of either or both sexes are found to experiment with each other for ways to produce the long-sought and vaunted sexual release through orgasm. Of course, the search for relief is found to include all the forms of perverse sexual activity of which humankind is capable, in its search for acceptance, love, and stimulation. We shall avoid trying to explain the extents and depths to which the human mind will go to produce satiation, for reasons probably well accepted by our readership: we are attempting to introduce something NEW.

"Our chief proposed purpose in providing you with any information at all on the sort of perversions we observe regularly employed is to cause the reader to note that there are unfamiliar and seldom experienced factors operating in the subtle mental and spiritual realms. When properly identified, cultivated, and then observed, in themselves they produce a higher and yet purer enjoyment than is possible to obtain solely at the physical and lower astral levels. The fact that there is any sexual feeling at all is a direct indicator of the presence of said currents, even though it is not necessary that they be recognized as currents to propagate the species.

"HOWEVER, once a person becomes sensitive enough, aware enough of those currents, he and she almost identically are able to heighten their enjoyment of Life itself through coursing said sex currents properly through the Chakra System during intercourse. For persons to become that much more aware of one's thoughts and feelings at all times, requires becoming increasingly aware of the similar thoughts and feelings of his associates and sexual partners.

"Not at all restricted to Western Churchdom, we offer here the use of Eastern (Oriental and Hindu) techniques, in which the human mind is trained carefully to make use of Thought Currents. The old masters of Raja (royal, or spiritual) Yoga were adept at teaching their students, their chelas, of the higher currents of life for use in consciousness expansion, healing, for levitation, and for materialization and de-materialization of physical objects, including their own human bodies. The use of such methods and training for political and sexual purposes was absolutely FORBIDDEN, and for at least one excellent reason, as we shall divulge.

"One name used to identify said kundalini current is 'The Serpent Fire.' Deliberate misuse of the Sacred Kundalini is almost universally deemed to be an open invitation to certain darker forces among Humanity, in an egoic sense seeking control over others, and therefore to be considered as black magic or voodoo. Now, let it be recognized that OUR position on the existence of magic at all, is that ALL IS MIND, ALL IS THOUGHT, but the USE and PURPOSE to which such forces are put determines whether said use is black or white, is spiritually legal, is constructive in the highest sense in not depriving another being of its basic right to Life, in not interfering with its individual expression of freedom.

"At the present date in the evolution of spirit-in-matter, it is well accepted that Mankind will not permit itself en masse to reexperience those older misuses of that Sacred Fire. He agreed to limit, not Man's capacity for Life, but his avenues to be used for its enjoyment. Thus the pendulum swings from one extreme to the other, from Puritanism to various forms of Hedonism. In Time Past, Mankind caused itself almost untold agony and karma by persistent misuse of the Creative Life Forces. In fact, it is still remembered, down deep in Collective Memory [the Akasha, shared by all because of ours, yours, and their connection through Universal Mind] that former cataclysms were generated, were certainly brought about, by collective and wide-scale misuse of that Kundalini Power, directed and misused as sexual energy. We speak of the Power To Love, the very same Sacred Fire of which the Bible speaks. Consider as a recorded example the cleansing power of Fire brought down upon Sodom and Gomorrah for its misuses of the creative act in Genesis 19:24.

"When we see people undertaking repetition of the ancient methods for attempting achievement of human orgasms, we are mindful that we are in the presence of old souls who do not remember their former glories, or who DO remember that there were former glories of some sort, but of which the details have been forgotten or suppressed, or who choose to rekindle old fires, in the face of the things and conditions they find themselves in today, in their present incarnation.

"Then by observing the widespread practice of misdirected spiritual energies, one can readily determine the TRUE STATE of Mankind, and by further observation, seeing then what Man has done to his sole surviving planet. One thus can easily determine the mental and spiritual state of Humankind at large.

"There are REALLY only a relatively few souls who have gained enough from living in human flesh to qualify for participation in our sort of through-the-veil self-christing ministry. We seek to help those special people to recognize themselves and to help them to graduate from the planet. Enough Time is still available to remove need for further incarnation here on Earth!

"In closing, let us become accepted as having taken advantage of the reader's curiosity long enough, hopefully that Mankind, each reader one by one, will undertake that fascinating and eventually highly rewarding search to understand himself as a Human Being. Then, for undertaking self purification and perfection, and consummating a lifelong pursuit to that end, he and she will both equally discover there is nothing in the Universe that he and she cannot duplicate, cannot have for themselves, INDEPENDENTLY of SEXUAL INTERCOURSE, and well beyond it in the sense of goodwill, accomplishments and fulfillment available.

"Then, if we have communicated adequately, if we have told you the full story, if in these words we were successful in stirring your further interest, we shall be gratified. The purposes of the Hierarchy for whom and with Whom we work shall be that much more swiftly accomplished.

"When you first saw this volume on the bookstore shelves in your quest for More Life Through Sex, you may not have recognized that we are using a contemporary Madison Avenue gimmick to offer an apparent tie-in between the sexual and the spiritual aspects of the Universe. But note carefully, please, that there are indeed available EXACTLY ALL those benefits and tie-ins we offered. A person's ability to persevere and experience them is where the rub comes.

"If a reader is unable to experience our claims, is unable to make them come true for himself, let the fault be found to lie in impatience, rather than in not having dedicated one's self and resources properly to study and apply the finer aspects of the Life of the Human Spirit! Surely it is already made clear that the Human Circumstance is but a mental creation. Man's environment was created for the sole purpose of enabling Spirit to experience Time and Matter and Space, as dimensions of Universal Creativity. Man is offered nearly limitless opportunity to grow in Mind, Love, and Grace, for pleasure, and at the same time to gain greatly in appreciation of SELF fulfilled on any and all of the highest levels.

"It is truly given that Earth as a way-station through the galaxy is but an introductory school, preparing graduates to enter the larger aspect of the Living Universe where awaits far greater joys than is even possible for us to describe. Doubt as to whether that claim is factual is in part indicated by your reluctance to accept as Truth our mouthings, and the teachings of all the ancient prophets and Avatars in your discernible past history in and out of the world's pulpits.

"Anyone who understands our message will surely begin immediately to learn more of how he or she has become trapped in flesh, and will then seek PROPER ways to rise above himself, above his addiction to egoic control, above his or her slavery to attempts at pleasure-seeking through manipulating Matter and Flesh.

"Note carefully, if you please, that it is in one's entrapment to pleasure . . . in one's ADDICTION to PLEASURE . . . that holds humanity in bondage to Time-Space-Matter, to the Great Wheel of Reincarnation.

"We find NOTHING AT ALL in this Universe to demonstrate or that tells Mankind that God limits or entraps Man in anything that Man can conceive or perceive. It is only *Mankind Itself* which is holding Itself to the many cycles of reincarnation, and therefore and thereby it is only when Mankind decides INDIVIDUALLY to look into our claims and validates them EACH FOR HIMSELF, that there will be found that greatest of all pleasure . . . Oneness with God, through oneness with ALL MANKIND.

"Man, in his attempts at finding bliss, is looking in the wrong places when he seeks ultimate satisfaction via his flesh vehicles. Seeking lasting pleasure via one's flesh is akin to making an automobile exceed the speed limits of prudence in his attempts at gaining thrills by gaining advantage over another similarly-equipped driver/owner. It makes about that much sense! Man is trying to take his jollies through short-term exploitation and mismanagement of his vehicles, not understanding that greater pleasures may be found in designing a better auto, or perfecting the one he has, or in planning and executing exciting trips to new vistas, learning how to use his present paid-for vehicle to bring greater joy to others who may be unable to own and operate a machine as fine as his.

"When enough of our message has rubbed off, you will know that you have entered upon the only pathway to bliss there is . . . OVERCOMING SELF. THAT occasion dawns as one comes to UNDERSTAND self . . . YOUR self.

"We hope and trust we have made our case, and that you are pleased to have found and read this, our latest attempt to reach the

Mind and Soul of Man. We TOO would bring you pleasure, but ours is apt to be a different or higher kind than you may have tried. Test OUR approach to obtaining Ultimate Pleasure . . . UNION with GOD!

"You can attain unto God-union through sexuality properly and fully expressed, remembering that sexuality itself is but one step on a long ladder. Acquisition and experience of bliss then requires clearing and cleansing and perfection in each level of the Human Experience . . . body, mind, and soul.

"In our assessment, Tantra Yoga is a step, a milestone along the way, but only that! To express Perfect Love does not require sexuality. "Amen."

CHAPTER

17

Have You Tried This?

"In our efforts to fulfill your anticipations in having purchased and perused this book, we shall make it easy for you to look in one place for the summary of every technique and practice which will guarantee yourself an improved sex life, including relationships more richly rewarding on any level, with or without physical sexual intercourse.

"Not necessarily in the order of importance to you, but certainly in the order of feasibility, in the order most likely to be of demonstrable value to you, are the following nine items. They will not necessarily be provided with in-depth supporting justification in this chapter, as many excellent and lengthy discourses are readily available in print elsewhere. We have selected and referenced a few in the Bibliography for your convenience."

1. Detoxify your blood stream.

"By your own effort, you can greatly enhance your sensitivity to the subtle psychic currents, and do much to balance the energy flows between your spiritual centers, the chakras. To achieve the best and permanent results requires your blood stream to contain proper levels of blood sugar and electrolyte, ensuring its optimum ability to carry oxygen to the heart muscle and brain systems, and to make maximum benefit from the raw and fresh foods you should be eating anyway. Daily ingestion of a cabbage or kale leaf serves as a powerful detoxifying agent. In other words, do whatever will enhance your physical health. Drink clean water and eat sparingly. Eliminate junk and processed foods, alcohol, drugs, and cease smoking and inhaling other air pollutants."

2. Enhance your general health.

"In addition to refining and perfecting your dietary intake, and eliminating addictions to chemically unbalanced foods and air pollutants, your general health is enhanced by undertaking regular physical exercise, consistent with your body build. Aim at producing longevity, resilience, and staying power. The objective is to establish normal blood flow through the body and mind, upgrading the ability of the bloodstream to carry fresh oxygen. Duplicating the 'jogger's high' is not necessary but would be found both exhilarating, and typical of a mind open to the higher levels of sensed alertness, with responsiveness to the higher realms. Many books, aerobic centers and private exercise programs, public TV programs, et cetera, are available that willingly and economically can abet your efforts at finding ways and easy accessible opportunities to undertake your lifelong body-fitness self-enhancement program, but you probably can do at home anything that needs to be done. In addition to the gains in mental alertness, you will marvelously restore your sexual 'staying power' with your sexual partner.

3. Take courses in Hatha Yoga and Tai Chi.

"Applicable both to males and females, regular programs will restore flexibility to your overall body-mind conditioning. For having a body that does not limit what your mind can imagine, you will become able to undertake more strenuous aspects of sexual enjoyment. It will keep your body able to support your general activities, including your sex life many more years than people ordinarily expect, and can prevent you from ever losing your ability to express affinity sexually."

4. Undertake conscious awareness development.

"We suggest especially that you undertake guided meditation and contemplation as attention-focussing exercises which will enrich your perception of the finer ethers and currents. You can gently build awareness of the energy flows that take place within and all around you, throughout, and between you and your partner. You will thus gain greatly in your ability to perceive through and behind the veil. Every thought and feeling of your loved one(s) will become yours to share, to further enjoy, and to mutually enhance pleasure, for being of a single Source.

5. Examine and clear your subconscious programming.

"Undertake an in-depth and long-term program of investigating and clearing your subconscious mind. Let yourself seek out and eliminate residual programs and attitudes that work against experiencing the higher subtler currents that provide the fullest enjoyment of life. Through renewing your minds, for thus perfecting yourself, you will perfect your relationships with God and Humanity, limited only to the extent and in the directions of what you are willing to consider."

6. Free yourself of FEAR.

"Becoming free of the fear of failure, detection, disease, and pregnancy will free you to LOVE. This is done partly by clearing your subconscious mind, and furthered by confining your sexual practices to proper circumstances. You must live up to *your own* highest value system. For their highest enjoyment, both partners must equally be willing and eager to participate responsibly in the sexual processes which God made available to Humanity. On taking proper care to learn and to practice the sorts of contact which are available, you can eliminate ineptitude, and change rape into rapture for you both.

7. Become free of GUILT

"Getting rid of buried feelings of Guilt has been made difficult, because present-era church and social systems seek to control the general populace through fear of God, fear of the police, fear of loss of income or status, through shame and fear of the Unknown, and of Authority in any or all forms. You must then strive diligently to learn to recognize when Guilt trips are being laid on you, and to see Life from a higher perspective. The Christ Life has no guilt, and yet is entirely appropriate and joyful, without any burden of man-made guilt. There is nothing constructive, nothing spiritual accomplished by carrying guilt. And when you cast out Fear, you *can* Love!"

8. Become psychic.

"Study to Know Yourself, and seek to understand what that means. Practice developing of your finer sensitivities, studying in a supportive environment. Learn what constitute the subtle aspects of Humanity, and learn to discern them. You can do this by becoming aware of your thoughts and feelings and the effects they have on you. At the same time, learn to become aware of the thoughts and feelings of the other persons in your environment, and of the extent to which they control yours and their activities.

"In other words, this is how you can become aware of what is already going on in your psyche, in the psyche of your loved ones and associates, and thus aware of the thoughts and feelings of all humanity. You then can take advantage of anything which will contribute to your higher levels of awareness of Life in its many forms. You will be able to produce a soothing and a healing environment, even in difficult social circumstances.

"When your observations are properly balance with Wisdom, which comes partly from Experience, you will attain Serenity, being then complete master of all you see."

9. Become what you know.

"Once you undertake expansion of your own consciousness, we believe you will find yourself learning other effective ways to enhance your overall enjoyment of Life, for willingly having undertaken discovery and practice of what lies ahead for you, as well as within you. Your relationships with Life, with your companions, and with Humanity in general will be greatly improved, and will be found to permit experiencing Life through the veil, a wonder-filled life existence above sex, and you will find that you do not miss the sexual aspect of human relationships.

"We suspect you have not yet seriously considered or realized the simplicity of these techniques, else you would not have needed this book. TRY THEM! You can ONLY WIN! Likewise, so can your partners, of whatever relationship. Proper preparation of mind, body, and soul are REQUIRED.

"OK?

"We rest our case."

18

Setting Yourself Free

"In the process of becoming all you can become, it is sometimes expeditious to have special help in cutting old bonds. Here is an excellent exercise in Creative Visualization. When practiced in sincerity and correctly, it dissolves certain ties that bond one person or soul to another. Its proper use brings immediate spiritual freedom to each party. It is capable, as well, of showing what a relationship had going for and against it if the user is able to perceive spiritual colors.

"To begin, stand erect in a quiet comfortable place and become centered. Take a few deep slow breaths to calm and energize your etheric body, breathing in pure Light. Visualize any clouds of tension leaving with each exhalation.

"Next, imagine the other person standing in front of you, facing you, perhaps three to five feet away. In a prayerful manner, in your speaking voice, address that person by name, the one from whom you wish to be freed, or to be set free from you. Announce clearly in spoken words that you are working with the Spirit of The Christ, to give each of you the freedom to live and move unencumbered of whatever chains that now tie you together. Know and affirm that as a result, you are creating a beautiful situation, releasing two trapped spirits to pursue their ultimate destinies, whether together or separated, and doing them no harm at all.

"Next, imagine a silvery communication line going from your lowest spiritual center (the 'root' or 'elimination' chakra) to the same center in the other person. Note whether that communication line is clear and clean, or if it wants to be smoky, clouded or covered over with a murky or gooey colored substance of some sort. If irregularity or discoloration are noted, let The Christ Light dissolve and sever that pathway or line: watch it disappear.

"Prayerfully complete that severance and acknowledge release of the connection at that point by invoking aloud 'Dear _____, in the name of the Father, Son, and Holy Ghost, I forgive you and release us to live to our highest good.'

"Please note that with some ties, it seems to help to do this three times, or until feeling that the release has been accomplished.

"Now, move up to the next pair of centers (chakras), connecting the reproductive organs and visualize a communication line running between them. Perhaps it too will be ill-defined, clouded over or hidden from view by darkness. Perceiving it as a red or dark red or brown color indicates that certain unnatural sexual matters may have been practiced, or that some unresolved matter is still remnant. Visualize the Light dissolving that connection, until it too is clear. As you see the connection cleared, pray aloud . . . 'Dear (name), In the name of The Christ Spirit I set us free. Amen!'

"Similarly establish a communication line connecting the third centers together (the spleen chakras). Let the nature of your connection on that level reveal itself to you. A muddy color indicates that there are unresolved emotional matters between you. Again, let the Light dissolve that psychic connection between you, while invoking the prayer 'Dear (Name), I release you and me from all subconscious ties. In the name of The Christ Spirit, Amen.'

"Once again, let a silver communication line be sent across to the person, connecting the heart centers. Observe its seeming coloration. If it is beautifully colored, clear in nature, then you may presume that you have established an excellent spiritual Love and rapport with that other person, that other incarnate soul. However, again, intone clearly the prayer 'Dear (Name), I release us on this level. In the name of

The Christ Spirit. Amen.'

"Now move up and establish a similar connection between your throat centers. If it is real enough to you, let its characteristics tell you what sort of relationship you have established with that other person on that level. Then intone again aloud something like: 'Dear (Name), I release you and me in the name of The Great Christ Spirit, and bless you. Amen.'

"Now move up to the brow chakras (the third-eye center) and imagine or visualize the spiritual connecting link between yours and the other person's brows. Observe the coloration of that connection to ascertain the sort of mind relationship you have established on that level with the other person. Again, let the Light dissolve the connection, until it too disappears completely. Again intone aloud . . . 'Dear (Name), in the name of The Christ Spirit, I set us both free. Amen!'

"Now move up and establish your psychic connection between the crown chakras (at the top of the head). Note whether the connection goes across from person to person, or if it seems to go up from each person, perhaps disappearing, or perhaps seeming to merge into God the Father. Note the coloration of that link, if you perceive any at all. Let The Christ Light again dissolve the mutuality of a person-to-person connection, knowing that you are now One through The Father, as you intone aloud the invocation, 'Dear (Name), in the name of Father, Son, and Holy Ghost, I decree that you and I are now free on all levels, and are One in the Father. Amen.'

"For this release process to be entirely effective, it is not necessary to perceive colors at all. According to your *belief* it is done unto you. OK?

"You are now unencumbered, unburdened from subjective attachments which may have been taking energy from your normal life activities, and making your relationships otherwise miserable.

"Depending on your ability to imagine or out-picture the connection, it may not be necessary to repeat the process a second or a third time. if it seems to be desirable to check upon your former connection, it is OK to do this process several times. Leave a period of several days between treatments, depending upon your sense of reality.

"However, almost immediately after performing this rite, you may sense the other person happily, swiftly, and freely moving away, perhaps ascending, but leaving you both as free agents. On later meeting them in person after having given yourselves this treatment, be prepared to be greeted with a fondness, an affectionate greeting, or at the very least, with a neutral detachment.

"REJOICE that you have such power!

"By observing the color and texture of each of the communication links between the chakras, you can discern much about the sort of relationship you have had or now have with your correspondent. This process releases the psychic ties between you and cleanses the good that may have been accumulated whenever generated. Bless your former relationship and give it to God.

"By undergoing this procedure, one often discovers that the other person becomes transformed in his attitude and appearance to you, and to each other. Without the former chains, each person is free to be his or her REAL SELF. You will probably end up loving them! Your former relationship with them will then be totally harmonious, even if you never see them again. At least, you have made a friend.

"Close by thanking The Christ Spirit for your mutual freedom.

"This can and should be done even for loved ones, renewing, clearing, and perfecting your relationships all around.

"OK?"

CHAPTER

19

Awakening Exercises

A person whose mental processes have been developed well enough to focus his or her attention is able to enter the metaphysical meditation state of consciousness, and working from there, may obtain the results we claim. This chapter describes processes by which one draws the Life Currents into his space and runs them through a course down from the top of the head, down the spine to the home of the kundalini, then turning the currents upward in a particular manner. Through these exercises a person becomes aware of the Life Currents, then becoming a healer by awakening his or her feeling self. One next becomes open to the sights and sounds of the Invisible Realms, awakening his Intuition, becoming a Knower. For having awakened one's higher capacities, it follows naturally that one develops the ability to experience all the feelings of sexuality DELUXE. When experiencing the sexual intercourse rite, the partners will reach heights of bliss not available to one whose centers are opened improperly, or in an unbalanced condition. For perfecting that awakening and balancing, it will not be necessary to have a physical presence, nor to experience physical touch or contact with one's gonads to reach said height of rapport.

"This is a fundamental introductory process, from which variations will become apparent as a person becomes aware of the current flows and of his or her centers. When the Student is ready, advance personalized variations become available, seemingly being self-suggesting. You are then not being shortchanged by undertaking these exercises in the order we present them. In other words, there is a natural order of things.

"We are using this particular approach for excellent reasons, so that you will circumvent (avoid) unbalancing your centers or incurring problems with living in the world, were your kundalini forces awakened improperly.

"First, a person is obliged to stand quietly, feet comfortably apart, with arms outstretched, left palm up, right palm down. With your eyes closed, imagine yourself appearing as a five-pointed star, your head in the top. Imagine you can feel a subtle tingling, the warmth of currents flowing into your left hand, going across to and out of the right hand palm and fingers. You may next sense (or imagine) the currents flowing into your left foot arch, up to the base of your spine, up to the heart area, and out the right arm, leaving the palm or fingers of the right hand. Next, imagine the currents coming into the left fingers and palm, coursing to the heart area and down the right leg, leaving the body through the right arch.

"Now, imagine those flows going on all at once. Note the relative balance in the amount of energy coursing in each path, observing if the currents gradually balance or equalize. Observe the processes gently for perhaps five minutes, while slowly counting to fifty. Then open your eyes and seat yourself until you feel rested enough to go on. Doing just this much is enough until you feel strong enough to continue with the next phase of the exercises. Just this much done twice daily is effective and is adequate for beginners.

"Now imagine a stream of golden-white light entering your heart from an unlimited source . . . God . . . out in front of you. Draw the current upwards into your head and move it along the left side of your neck, into your left shoulder, arm, and leave it in a swirl in the fingers of the left palm. Then return to the Heart center, drawing in another quantity of golden-white energy. Take it to the top of the head, moving it down the right side of your head, neck, shoulders and arm, leaving it in a swirl in the right palm. Now imagine drawing another charge of Life Energy into the heart, lifting it to the crown and conducting it down the left side of the spine and leg, leaving it in the left arch. Again, draw in more Life Energy into the Heart center, taking it to the top of the head, the crown chakra. Now draw it down the right side of the neck and torso, down the right leg, and leave it in the right arch. A fifth time, draw in more Life energy into the Heart Center and draw it up to the crown, then spiralling it down to the lower tip of the spine. Hold it there, warming the area while intoning AUM for three breaths. Then draw the current around to the front of the body, dwelling briefly on each center as you close by drawing it up to the crown chakra again.

"Sense yourself being filled with LIFE, with sensitivity, with a tingling or glowing feeling of well-being. Offer a short affirmation or prayer of gratitude that all is well in your universe space. Note how well and charged up you feel. Slowly open your eyes, carrying this feeling with you as you go about your normal affairs.

"A time will come when the down-flow of Life current will want to go down the left side of your spine and rise again to the crown chakra along the right side of your spine (the Ida and the Pingala). For the present time, just observe that flow to take on whatever if any colors and pathway deviations it may take, coaxing it along as necessary.

"Later, when the current flows smoothly, without seeming to hang-up at one or another chakra, you will find the strength of the current increasing. When that time comes, allow the up-going current to rest briefly in each center/chakra, allowing each center to show you what color it is. When things are "right," you will note the colors of the rainbow as you go from bottom to top. The overall integrated color will be the white Christ Light. You will find yourself able to diffract the Christ Light even as a prism exposes the constituent colors of white light, letting each color find its proper chakra.

"When and as you reach the perfection available by this method of awakening your highest capacities for experiencing and expressing Life, you will find yourself able to transcend the bliss available heretofore only through sexual intercourse, but you may find your new joys so much higher than provided only by intercourse that you no longer really want to interrelate sexually. You literally will have the best of both worlds, the Higher and the Incarnate worlds.

"Of interest to many will be finding hang-ups or blocks to current flows. A well trained clairvoyant or psychic psychologist will be able to discern the nature of the hang-ups and help remove them. Most of the time it will be found that old attitudes and programs are interfering, blocking present-time current flows. It should not surprise you to find that old vows of Poverty, Chastity, and Obedience taken in past-life monasteries and convents will still be operating. One then has to release himself from those old vows, freeing the subconscious mind from one's old obligations. Sometimes the blocks will be found to be Fear, Guilt, or a powerful decision never again to touch a particular person for what he or she did or did not do in a previous incarnation. Sometimes it will be found that a lack of self-esteem is preventing a person from enjoying a life normally otherwise available.

"Then far from being trivial exercises, developing sensitivity to and awareness of the powers of one's soul or psyche is at the root of experiencing Tantra Yoga, and to what lies further on for the spiritual aspirant. Here methods are being made available to open up the chakras, methods that have been available only in the Mystery Schools.

"Our approach and techniques are being released here in one place for perhaps the first time in centuries. Not all persons will benefit equally or develop at the same rate, but all can and will achieve the ultimate goal of Perfect Oneness with any one person or all persons, finding self then christed through having perfected one aspect of himself, and expanding that to awakening his total self.

"Is not the attainment of Bliss the goal of all religions?

"We rest."

CHAPTER

20

Total Encounter Therapy

"When it comes to the ability to express one's self enthusiastically, with total abandon, to converting Life Force into those processes producing orgasm, let it be recognized clearly that the capacity of the human female for responding cannot be transcended, nor hardly be matched. Not having to produce the human sperm, being instead the receiving terminal or receptacle for same, enables said human female to focus her full attention on directing those energy flows to the experience of prolonged pleasure. Then those females whose constitution and health permit more or less unlimited receipt and expression of Life Force are able to respond with a sense of fulfillment far longer, more intensely, and much more frequently than can nearly any human male incarnate since the Golden Era of Greece.

"But most females do not know of their capability! Most females would try for it if they were uninhibited, felt free to do so. Some are engaging promiscuously looking for some vaguely remembered condition which they inwardly sense can be theirs through sexual intercourse of the proper sort, or with the right male. As with most males, their urgencies to perform or to please are often proportional to their degree of stress.

"Even mildly active females are often referred to as being oversexed, and are sometimes called 'nymphs.' But those labels are affixed by males, who are themselves generically unable to approach the unlimited levels of female expression. By middle-age, the typical human male is infrequently able to deliver more than one or two loads of sperm to his waiting female. In cases where the male is of unusually fine physical conditioning, and has awakened enough of his sacred Kundalini Fires, he is still likely only able to match the so-called 'normal' females.

"As we occasionally note relative to humans losing their fires of youth, it is the female who is most apt to be found conditionable, to retain and express their capacity for frequent orgasmic response.

"There is a second side to the coin of unlimited sexual expression. That other side can represent females who are frigid, who cannot make love under any conditions, try as they might.

"We have a therapy by which both extremes can gain release. Slight modification of the same basic therapy will release persons of either sex who are addicted to either extreme form of sexual expression. In other words, we have tools useful in removing subjective blocks as causes for several types of sexual dysfunction.

"Even so, despite their generic potentials, we recognize that the human female orgasm is infrequently experienced and rarely involuntary, whereas male orgasmic response by design encourages generation and discharge of sperm, assuring human reproduction. Orgasm production in human females is not required to accomplish reproduction, but good genital feelings surely encourage participation in sexual intercourse. Female orgasm production then can be an acquired state, and when observed clairvoyantly, a latent susceptibility for orgasmic response can be seen to be brought forward from earlier lives. Some aristocratic societies still cultivate that capability, and have developed it as an art form, is much to be sought. Some primitive societies destroy that capacity by clitoral circumcision. [Margaret Mead]

"Male skill in satisfying a female is then both a desired condition and an acquired ability, and a major factor in assessing marital compatibility and/or dissatisfaction, especially when the female is aware of the ecstasies available.

"We shall address our remarks today at identifying some of the basic reasons why humans of either sex sometimes find themselves unsatiated by one or two normal orgasms, why some females do not require or cannot achieve orgasmic responses, and why some do not achieve lasting satisfaction from any number of orgasms.

"Many persons of either sex consider themselves unloved or incapable of being loved when judged solely by the intensity or frequency of sexual intercourse, with or without orgasm. We presume here only that such persons desire and are willing to pursue further study and take specific action for improvement or alleviation of such activity, whether for personal need, pleasure, procreation or for profit.

"Our present approach merges Tantra Yoga with Psychotherapy. By including carryovers from Judeo-Christianity, we come out with the best of all worlds, and a therapy to achieve same. For convenience, and to help to clarify matters, we begin by identifying the extremes, going from persons who experience endless orgasms at will but have no sense of fulfillment, to persons who cannot derive satisfaction from any amount of sexual activity. Other than to those who engage professionally, we refer primarily to those who are *addicted* to the *process* of sexual intercourse, usually to those who are seeking fulfillment. Unidentified as being of little interest are most relatively normal persons in between!

"For the highly active human male in the USA we reserve the word 'Stud.' The comparable female is called 'Nymph.' In either case there are several criteria, not necessarily related, for judging addiction to the sexual processes: the depth, the quantity, and the type of participation. Quality as an outcome does not weigh here, and is not always achieved, however much sought-after as an outcome.

"First, we shall consider the element of human diet. Following that, we shall discuss several criteria by which a soul-self sometimes blocks its search for acceptance and approval, considered from the point of view of lifting a low sense of self-esteem. Thirdly, we address the factor of unrealistic and unmet expectations believed necessary to be satisfied by the sexual expression itself.

"We presume, of course, that the ABILITY and CAPACITY for quantitative orgasmic *or* non-orgasmic expression are limited primarily by the state of one's physiological health, but perhaps equally so by psychological or/and mental health, augmented by the developed capacity available for Kundalini current flow.

"Using metaphysical jargon, we try to speak *quantitatively* of the extent to which the lower chakras in the human aura or psyche are awakened to the Life Current or kundalini flows. Open chakras and excellent health and good attitudes all contribute to and enhance the higher levels of sexual activity. It stands to reason that lacking said health, having poor mental conditioning, and low levels of orgasmic response, if any at all, may include lack of suitable partners with whom to practice the sexual arts. Much depends on one's value system and opportunity for regular sexual expression. Otherwise lacking suitable partners capable of inflicting or fulfilling strong desires, one will seek expression in homosexuality, abuses, or in other outlets such as overeating, in fantasy, in excessive use of alcohol, and perhaps in use of aphrodisiacs or drugs of various kinds.

"When we come to the matter of *qualitative* performance, we necessarily consider the degree of awakening and balance of the upper three chakras as represented in the Menorah, and in the higher Lights Before The Throne [Revelations 1:12].

"In regard to the place that dietary factors enter into human sexual expression, let it be recalled that 'humans become what they eat.' Perhaps not literally, in the sense that we take on the physical shape of said vegetable or animal, but that the human psyche does indeed become congested with etheric-plane animal by-products. Ingestion of deceased animal carcasses clouds the eater's mental capacity, and tends to transfer the animal's emotional responses but lightly unabated. Growth hormones are widely known to be carried from the body of the slain animal directly into the human bloodstream, where they operate but little affected by the dietary transfer.

"The fear-chemicals (adrenaline) produced in the animal at the time of its slaughter later influence the human autonomic system, controlling the eater's attitudes and automatic or programmed reactions similarly to the emotions and attitudes already contained in the psyche of said ingested animal-body flesh. The animal's emotional state is also carried along in the finer ethers which constitute the desire body of the slain animal. *These processes can be observed by personal trial and diet control!*

"At the high end of the spectrum of human soul purity we observe the vegetarian psyche to have an aura entirely free from animal soul influences, and free from animal chemistry. Instead, the subtle higher essence is filled energized with the pure auric essences of properly grown and properly prepared fresh fruits and vegetables. Let it be stated here that seldom is there any inability or lack of interest in human sexual expression on the part of human vegetarians. Indeed, let it be noticed that rarely is there a preoccupation with sexuality in such persons, as that derived eating animals and animal products. However, psychological sources of addiction or sexual dysfunction can still be at play, even among long-term vegetarians.

"We again note that over-ingestion of alcohols, and eating large quantities of spices and certain strong herbs, while in themselves of vegetarian origin, can also stimulate sexual responses. Alcohols and spices have long been cultivated for their alleged aphrodisiac propensities. Olfactory, visual and auditory stimulation also have strong and traceable connections with the arousal of humans to sexual activity. No surprise that exterior arousal is noted when sensitive areas of the human sexual body are stimulated, as by the sort of clothing worn, and by deliberate contact.

"Let us consider next that psychological factors also influence strongly one's demands for or inhibitions from sexual satisfaction. Perhaps the strongest of these is the passion experienced as an excruciating need to be recognized and accepted, to the extent that one says in effect . . . "If I do this thing . . . if I have sex with that person, maybe they will love me, like me, live with me, take care of me, or recompense me in some way, even if for a short time: that would be better than what I am getting now!"

"Here again we have a dichotomy. The human male is classically interested in physical relief through sexual expression, after which he forgets the instrument of his deliverance, perhaps going on to the next opportunity to satisfy himself, or just rolling over and going to sleep.

"On the other hand, the female may have been intent on satisfying some need of her own through sexual expression, with or without necessarily experiencing the orgasm as a payoff. As stated, relatively few members of the world of human females regularly experience orgasm, and perhaps most of those who do so use self-administered processes, more than through the help of a cooperative male or female.

"Then, especially noted here is the phenomenon that most females over the world submit dutifully to their inevitable rape, in which their male counterpart, lover or husband, perhaps not knowing any better himself, pursues pleasure by submitting to the mechanical processes of intercourse. With good fortune, said females will be treated gently, enabling said sexual process, temporarily at best, to reflect or transfer the feelings of being loved or appreciated. But too often it is quite the reverse, in which a female will be subjected to beatings, suffering humiliation and pain in various manners to enable the male to arouse his perhaps otherwise flagging libido. Surely, the natural sexual processes themselves do release a strong flow of feelings, but to some males, use of fantasy and physical torture are the only ways they are able to attain and maintain an erection. Of sadomasochistic matters we do not intend here to discourse further, other than to recognize ways to release the resulting psychic blockages which *females* sometimes build to cope with such mistreatment.

"What works for one human will work equally well for members of the opposite sex.

"We proceed next to consider that sexual favors often are used as bribes to influence or gain control over some giver of gifts. We do not know just how frequently fathers, mothers, sisters and other friends consciously instill in their fledgling daughters or sons the belief that sexuality is a commodity, a medium of exchange, to be sold to the highest bidder. How skillfully one negotiates his physical favors determines how high he rises in the world. The best prostitutes frequently become idols of the cinema; some are honored and revered in high places.

"You may already be aware of the prevalence in high places of Geishas and the best prostitutes, and know the extent they are used as spies by the military, politicians, and executive salesmen to court their accounts.

"Children, both boys and girls, are used by mothers and fathers, by bosses and policemen, by racketeers, by preachers who have not found a satisfactory relationship with Life, by anyone in a position to dispense favors for protection, to obtain a meal-ticket or a roof or clothing. Even at an early age, use is made of the ages-old process of bargaining with sexuality as a reward, AND AS AN INSTRUMENT FOR SELLING OR BUYING LOVE.

"During most expressions of sexuality, pure love as such indeed has very little to do with the actualities of expressing Affinity. Sexuality has become a SYMBOL of Love. Then, persons low in self-esteem often find themselves easily, or explicably victimized in relying on said sexual expression as a way to gain a sense of self-worth on ANY level.

"Let it be noted that the lower one's sense of self-esteem, the more desperately is said seeker of approval likely to create opportunities for using sexual intercourse to gain or to restore flagging spirits. Inwardly he or she is saying . . . "when I am being laid, everything is alright," and it seems to work for a few hours or days. Until something else comes along to upset one's equilibrium, things go relatively peacefully.

"Consider the problems raised for a person in great need of Love, who finds herself or himself blocked from participating in the usual sexual and other forms of chemical or physical abuses, or blocked by strong value systems inflicted or implanted in the subconscious mind. These may be some of the sorriest cases we have experienced, since those same persons are thereby also blocked for access to the higher levels of Mind from whence could come their succor.

"NOW . . . consider the plight of persons afflicted with combinations of all these categories as compelling causes for their unusual sexual activity. Persons whose economic situation and life style causes their dietary practices to be flawed, who are more or less desperate for being loved, wanted, lived with, supported, consoled, or even only noticed.

"In such cases, note also that the condition of one's physical apparatus or youthfulness both limits and dictates the form and degree of addiction available or taken up to satisfy the basic ego need!"

THERE IS A WAY OUT!

"We now explore and offer a way to bring genuine help and release for sexually distraught persons, to victims of whatever cause and form of abuse. To those persons who can still respond, we offer help to examine their psyche in a manner that will relieve the psychic and psychological causes of most of said afflictions. We describe a new approach, one that very few professional therapists are able to apply successfully, so strong are the inner fires and forces at work in seeking to provide satisfaction through physically expressed sexuality. The therapist SHOULD be clear!

"A therapist who is clear psychologically in some department of his or her incarnate experience, a situation rarely observed among today's doctorally-degreed practitioners, can indeed be of tremendous value to an aching client, in that same area. However, if said therapist is *not* clear, or is less clear than his client, then application of our method will probably implicate both parties, adding to the woes of both the therapist and the client. INDEED, insufficient resolution of a counselor's personal case is immediately obvious to us as the basic cause of why so many academically trained therapists become sexually involved with their clientele . . . they have not experienced resolution of their *own* Sex and Love hang-ups.

"Implicated immediately is the human ego and its buried banks of programming, rather than any satan-like figure, with the attendant difficulty in attempting to clear the subconscious feeling-self with conventional head-trip out-of-the-book intellectualized therapies.

"For what follows, we necessarily presume that the Therapist has cleaned up his or her own case, and has become master of his or her own soul or psyche to the extent that he can guide a client successfully through the idealized processes now to be divulged."

THE THERAPY

"Ideally, the therapist and the client will be lying nude on a king-sized bed in this phase of depth therapy. In practice it is wiser to let the Therapist and the Client become disrobed to the level of Bikinis and shorts, then lying semi-nude on the equivalent of a king-sized bed. Let the surroundings be secure and comfortable. Let both parties lie face up, side by side, with arms and legs spread comfortably. Let the Therapist lie on the left side of the bed, the client to his or her right.

Let the counselor's right toes/foot/leg be in contact comfortably with the left foot/leg/ankle of the client. Let them similarly hold hands, fingers gently intertwined. Let the lights be dimmed to the point where the client's attention is easily focussed on mental imagery when hovering in the reverie state. If soothing background music is available, let it inspire reverie but not be strong enough to be distractive. A faint perfume or incense may support a mood of rightness, of peacefulness and safety.

"Several minutes of initializing relaxation processes may be found of value, such as slow deep breathing, inhaling the essence of Peace, so that the client feels protected and safe. Not at all out of place at the outset is a mutually expressed short prayer and affirmation for the greatest good to result from each particular session.

"After the client has gained experience in entering and working in a reverie state of mind, assist the client in gaining awareness of his own energy flows, learning how to contact, view and experience his recordings. On reaching a state of stability in the mechanics of the process, and when general comfort in the session relationship is gained, it will be feasible for the Therapist to ask the Client to imagine a time (or times) when he or she was well accepted, when things were going well. On achieving suitable responses, on being able to report what is contained in the scenario, on what the feelings are of the participants, thank him and ask him to let go of it. When the client reports that the scenario has vanished, ask him to look for another sort of scenario, a distressful incident. Let the client report details of the scenario as they become apparent, seeking to identify the central figure, someone who may be committing some sort of indignity, perhaps attempting to control the client by threatening to withhold approval. That central villain may be your mother, father, teacher, boy or girl friend, uncle, minister, etc.

"As an aid to visualizing the scenario, ask the client to describe his clothing, his approximate age, where he is, and what sort of situation of approval or censure he is experiencing, and how he feels about it. Ask the client to keep looking into the scenario for what is occurring, reporting shifts in how he feels, and to report similarly shifts in the feelings perceived by the villain.

"When both the therapist and the client are subjectively tuned in on the proceedings, this state of affairs can decently be extended into areas of sexual trauma. Continue with the comfortable physical juxta-position on the bed, maintaining an awareness of the potential for compromise, but doing nothing to stimulate or further enhance a sexual response. If a block or lack of response is experienced, a gentle abdominal massage will often liven things up. From time to time, ask the client to report how they feel NOW, and use the response to gauge proper follow-on activity.

"By carefully perceiving, listening to the response, the therapist will readily know how rapidly and in what direction to proceed. Expect the first few sessions to be used in gaining client confidence in the therapist, and in use of the procedures for entering and working in the reverie state, coming to feel safe when working in such an exposed state of body and mind, in 'I have nothing to hide' circumstances.

"When a suitable level of confidence is reached, when client awareness of their respective nudity has become accepted and of little concern, it may become beneficial to rely on touch more pervasive than hand-holding to support the client through difficult scenes. These include times like when confronting recordings of bestial encounters, rapes, and childbirth trauma. For the process to be effective, the client should readily review and steadily report whatever seems appropriate to the old scenarios being reevaluated, even if done cautiously.

"The feeling to be established and maintained is the state of mind of being safe, protected, while not symbolically COVERING or HIDING ANYTHING. One quickly learns to accept and experience the concept that in the Light of Truth, NOTHING can or needs be hidden. Being thusly guided in being totally facilitates total recall, becoming able to probe at will into all things and situations exactly as they are recorded on the Akasha. THAT was the objective for having developed this method of Total Encounter, for releasing sexual aberra-tions and/or addictions.

"After a few successful sessions of this deep therapy, a transforma-tion in the client's attitudes will be apparent. The client has gained a new ability, a refreshing freedom, a spontaneity of response in his or her human relationships.

"When the client is comfortable with this form of supine confrontation it will be optimally feasible for the skilled Therapist to deepen the Akashic Search for specific types of engrams, and to intensify the use of fully conscious in-depth reverie regression processes here being suggested and described.

"Our experience enables us to hold the position that hypnosis as usually practiced is unnecessary in this work, contributes nothing, and usually runs counterproductively to the aims and purposes herein described, which are release from . . . by CONSCIOUS discharge of . . . the sources of subconscious distressful recordings.

"On specific orders from The Hierarchy Who delivered this technology, USE OF HYPNOSIS IN ANY FORM IS FORBIDDEN. Therapist and client alike reading these words shall recognize the message that use of hypnosis blocks Hierarchical access and participation in these processes, so that advocating hypnosis is not in accord with this method of releasing an ailing psyche. Purely CONSCIOUS and VOLUNTARY perception, participation, and pervasion must at all times be the modus operandi.

"By consistently asking the Client to observe, to feel, and to evaluate the circumstances of each imaged or recalled event and situation, the Client will readily be guided in confronting what has been transpiring in the original recorded (or mocked-up) meetings with his or her antagonists.

"Noting and carefully verbalizing the FEELINGS of each participant in the inner imaged scenario is important, for release lies in REEVALUATING and NEUTRALIZING the recorded FEELINGS, whether TRUE, or 'just imagined.' The subconscious mind often cannot tell the difference between subjective reality and objective reality. In just this sort of processing is wherein release is obtained from the roots to said addiction.

"The time will come when nude confrontation is no longer needed, so can be dispensed with. Said time will be recognized, when, on running The Process throughout any relationship the subconscious programming produces no present-time traumatic reactions, each troublesome recording or engram having become neutral. To reach that state of mind the client usually needs to have been run through some of the standard banks of possible scenarios. [See the Suggested Reading section.]

"The therapist will do well to balance his heavy therapy by interspersing questions seeking the opposite form of experience, like "Look for a time when you were receiving the sort of approval you like! Tell me how it seems to you. What form is it taking *now*? Describe what is going on, and do not let it change."

"The Therapist then guides the Client through every aspect of each troublesome relationship, until the client has become neutral to the originally troublesome sexual or other aberrational and/or addictive relationship, and is again in control of himself. The client's Reactive Mind will no longer be triggered inappropriately in contemporary social life.

"Practitioners skilled in Perlsian Gestalt Therapy can lead a client through our Total Encounter proceedings more rapidly than most others now being used for clearing the Akasha.

"The therapist may find other unrelated buried trauma, seemingly triggered by some commands, but should handle them similarly, as they probably bear directly on some undiscovered aspect of the client's spiritual welfare, else they would not come up.

"Much energy will be found to have accumulated in the subconscious addiction-related recordings, to have become trapped and unavailable for the normal life processes. Viewed clairvoyantly, such past-life scenes often appear clearly in the imagery of the client, and require skilled approach to neutralization. Or, a particularly painful trauma may resist viewing at all!

"If a particular trauma is sealed off, resists being reviewed, it may be possible to access the area by probing in kindred areas to try to identify in what related area of the client's feelings are not yet being blocked. Sooner or later, such areas can be released by a general search through the Akasha, using a standard list of human engrams already discovered [see Bibliography]. Electronic technology being made available through this channel usually will identify the block clearly. ["Electronic Aides To The Psychotherapist," PhD dissertation in Electrical Engineering by Dr. A. C. Lytle, PhD, soon to be published for public access.]

"A therapist may begin by looking for egoic blind spots, approaching his client's recordings from the fringes, looking for tics and signs of maltreatment, torn clothing, bloody hands, torture, burning, hangings, imprisonment, illness, and starvation. Sometimes investigating for cannibalism will provide insight and release through permitting going around the unprotected edges of the recorded trauma.

"If the client is skilled enough at using Creative Imagery, assist him in finding trauma recordings by looking for tough steel-blue or solid black areas and manipulating them.

"Bombarding a blocked area with slivers of golden light eventually will soften most areas enough to permit contact with their hideous contents, then making possible their release by neutralization. Other methods for dissolving blocked areas have been perfected, but it is not our present purpose to discourse on general soul therapy. That disclosure is reserved for the above dissertation, to be published through these same channels.

"Whether of the same sex or opposites, both the client and the therapist should recognize the potential for 'falling in love,' in the sense that for having shared success in achieving higher levels of awareness, it is not at all surprising that a sexual reward by 'transfer' might suggest itself as an ultimate form for expressing mutual appreciation.

"HOWEVER, it is important to note that strong feelings of Judeo-Christian client-counselor affinity are best expressed through simple TOUCH, observing the current or energy flows involved, rather than through genital contact. In other words, for best results, the therapist must be skilled in observing, passively resisting, or by withholding or diverting Tantric energy flows. The client must similarly become able to accept the implications of her or his new state of being. The pressures to express Love sexually which result from successful therapy can then be translated and experienced again on higher levels by BEING AWARE of those energy flows, perceiving and enjoying them, mutually exploring the new freedoms attained by unblocking psychic energy deposits and communication lines.

"It should be and usually will be found that successful Total Encounter therapy, conducted with the proper intent, decorously understood and conducted, will yield unexpected forms of relevancy through emergence of a new and higher level of affinity than the Client has as yet experienced, even sustained at the levels of sublimity of previous orgasmic attainment. By this approach, in this manner, the end result is assuredly the emergence of the released soul as another salvaged spirit incarnate in Materiality, and thus made available for further ongoing, or/and direct service to releasing other entrapped souls.

"Engaging in sexual intercourse after such exalted sessions may be permitted, but should not be used as any sort of payment, because so MUCH INDEED derives from preserving the personal value systems of both the Therapist *and* the Client, preserving the psychological space between them. The goal of these sessions is then to gain a fulfilled sense of Self Esteem as Human Spirit incarnate, freeing said client from the old hang-ups and classical methods for attempting to taste TRUE LIFE. It should be the client's experience that he/she will NO LONGER NEED TO rely on expression through former addictions. Sexual intercourse will still be a wonderful means to express affinity, but will be found to be an unsatisfying method for expressing the highest levels of fulfillment, unless used to prepare a body for an incoming soul.

"Tantric Yoga is then properly seen to be a high but an intermediate step, although a delightful and perhaps necessary step along The Way to attainment of individual Christing. Having reached a state of Clear permits the freed soul to experience genuine multilevel Love, likely preferring it to sexual love. This will be found true, partly because it is SO EASY and so rapidly possible to exchange and/or express Love through the energy flows of simple touch, an embrace . . . even through deep eye contact. It is hardly worth the effort to set up a sexual liaison when TRUE LOVE at the highest levels is shared so effectively by mind-to-mind or Soul to Soul contact.

"When ending a series of Total Encounter sessions, if feasible, appropriate, and acceptable to the client, the therapist and the client should embrace respectfully, cautiously, delightfully savoring the warmth of each other's presence. It will be found unnecessary and unwise to allow genital coupling. All through this it is vitally important that the

energy flows be sensed, feeling the new IMPERSONAL ACCEP-
TANCE, TRUST, the SAFETY, and the APPROVAL . . . the
LOVE . . . of each for the other. Orgasmic dividends, while available,
should not be felt required!

"Enough guidance in principle and practice is presented here to
enable an experienced mental health practitioner, one who himself or
herself has reached a state of Clear in the area of Relationships, to
undertake and gain the benefits of Tantra Yoga and beyond, both for
himself and his clientele.

"Thusly, the Tantric experience can be merged with the process
of the ultimate and overall Spiritualization of the human soul.

"THIS IS NOT A PROCESS FOR AMATEURS.

"We rest."

Suggested Reading

The following works are suggested for their ability to encourage correlation and integration between the Sexual, Metaphysical, Religious, Medical, and the Psychological views of Man. Each work, of course, will lead to others.

1. *Secrets of Western Tantra,* subtitled *Sexuality and The Middle Path* by Dr. Christopher Hyatt, PhD, FALCON PRESS, 1989

2. *Tantra, Spirituality, and Sex* by Bhagwan Shree Rajneesh available through The Dawn Horse Book Depot, 916 NE 64th St., Seattle, Washington 98115

3. *The Road Less Traveled* by M. Scott Peck, M.D., A Touchstone Book by Simon and Schuster, Rockefeller Center, 1230 Avenue of the Americas, New York, N. Y. 10020

4. *The URANTIA Book* published by The Urantia Foundation, 533 Diversey Parkway, Chicago, Illinois 60614 (A marvelous resource

5. *Male Sexuality* by Bernie Zilbergeld, PhD, Batam Books 1978; Little, Brown, & Company, 34 Beacon St., Boston, MA 02106. (A contemporary classic)

6. *From Bethlehem to Calvary,* subtitled *The Initiations of Jesus* by Alice A. Bailey Published by Lucis Publishing Company, New York.

7. *Discipleship In The New Age* by Alice A. Bailey Same as above. (A channeled classic by The Tibetan)

8. *The Labours of Hercules* by Alice A. Bailey As above. (Channeled by The Tibetan: The Labors aired)

9. *The Aquarian Conspiracy, Personal and Social Transformation in the 1980's* by Marilyn Ferguson: published by J. P. Tarcher, Inc., Los Angeles, Distributed by St. Martin's Press, N.Y.

10. *Self Esteem, Overcoming Inferiority Feelings* by C. G. Osborne Abingdon Press, Nashville, Tennessee

11. *The Truth About Creative Visualization* by The Llewellyn Editorial Staff. Published by Llewellyn Publications, P. O. Box 64383–353, St. Paul, Minnesota 55164–0383

12. *Self Analysis* by L. Ron Hubbard, (1987) published by Bridge Publications, Inc., 1414 No. Catalina Street, Los Angeles, CA 90027. (A fine collection of engrams)

13. *So YOU want to be A CHANNEL!* by A. C. Lytle, Jr., PhD FALCON Press 3660 No. 3rd Street, Phoenix, AZ 85012 (channeled by the same guides Who channel *this* book) (Available from most USA Metaphysical Book stores)

14. *Personal Power Through Awareness* by Sanaya Roman. H. J. Kramer Inc., Publishers, P. O. Box 1082. Tiburon, California 94920

15. *How To Develop Your ESP Power* by Jane Roberts: Pocket Books Division of Simon & Schuster, Inc. 1230 Avenue of the Americas, New York, N. Y. 10020

16. *Global Mind Change* Willis Harman, PhD. Published by Knowledge Systems, Inc., 7777 West Morris Street, Indianapolis, Indiana 46231 (A contemporary study of world-mind shifts.)

17. *Optimum Child, Developing Your Child's Fullest Potential Through Astrology.* by Gloria Star, reached through The Llewellyn New Times, P. O. Box 64383–740, St. Paul, Minnesota 555164–0383

18. *DIANETICS, The Modern Science of Mental Health* by L. Ron Hubbard, Bridge Publications, Inc., 1414 North Catalina Street, Los Angeles, CA 90027 (A classic in mind dynamics)

19. *Closing of the American Mind* by Allan Bloom, Simon & Schuster Rockefeller Center, 1230 Avenue of the Americas, New York, N. Y. 10020 (A contemporary study of social processes)

20. *Being A Woman* Dr. Toni G. Grant, PhD, Random House, New York, 1988, (A psychologist's points of view)

21. *SPIRIT SPEAKS* Magazine, Vol I Issue 6, "Love and Sexuality" pub by SPIRIT SPEAKS, P. O. Box 84304, Los Angeles, CA 90073 (An excellent source of Hierarchical views)

22. *The Inner Life,* by C. W. Leadbeater: The Theosophical Publishing House, 306 W. Geneva Road, Wheaton, IL 60187

23. *Loving Each Other* by Leo Buscaglia, Fawcett, New York (A classic adapted to college-age persons)

24. *Christ Enthroned In Man* by Cora Fillmore, UNITY School of Christianity, Lee's Summit, MO 64065 (contains powerful chakra opening exercises).

25. *The Kama Sutras of Vatsayayana,* translated by Sir Richard Burton, (Available through The Dawn Horse Book Depot) (A classic collection on ancient sexology)

26. *Healing Love Through The Tao* by Mantak Chia & Maneewan Chia (Available through The Dawn Horse Depot loc cit.) (An advance Chinese philosophy of Love.)

27. *Sexual Energy Ecstasy* by David Alan Ramsdale & Ellen Darfman. Available through The Dawn Horse Book Depot, 916 NE 64th Street, Seattle, Washington 98165

28. *Sexual Palmistry* by Roman Packer, The Aquarian Press, Wellingborough, Northamptonshire, England, 1986.

29. *Noetic Sciences Review* Quarterly Magazine by The Institute of Noetic Sciences, 475 Gate Five Road, Suite 300, P. O. Box 909 Sausalito, California

30. *Therapeutic Trances, The Cooperation Principle in Ericksonian Hypnotherapy* by Stephen G. Gilligan, 1987, Brunner/Mazel, Inc., 19 Union Square, New York 10003

31. "Ecstacy Through Tantra" by Dr. John Mumford, 1988, Llewellyn Publications, P.O. Box 64383, St. Paul, MN 55164-0383

32. "Dr. Ruth's Guide To Good Sex" by Dr. Ruth Westheimer, Warner Books, 1983, 666 Fifth Ave., New York, NY 10103

33. "Sexual Solutions" by Michael Castleman, 1980 Touchstone Division of Simon Schuster, 1230 Avenue of the Americas, New York, NY 10020

34. *The Sensuous Lover's Guide* by Dr. Kenneth Ray Stubbs. The Sensuous Lover, Box 67-0A, Larkspur, CA 94939-0067

35. *ESO-Extended Sexual Orgasm . . . An Illustrated Guide* by Brauer & Brauer, Warner Books, Inc., 666 5th Avenue, New York, NY 10103

36. *For Yourself—The Fulfillment of Female Sexuality* by Barbach, Doubleday/Anchor, 666 5th Avenue, New York, NY 10103

37. *Solutions—Practical and Effective Antidotes for Sexual and Relationship Problems* by Bandler, Future Pace, Inc., P.O. Box 1173, San Rafael, CA 94915

38. *Courses in Tantric Development* available from The New Age Workshop, Inc., PO Box 7000-618, Redondo Beach, CA 90277